cases and projects in international management

For Maggie, Chuu and Deng

cases and projects in international management

R ICHARD M EAD

BLACKWELL
Business

First published 2000

2 4 6 8 10 9 7 5 3 1

Blackwell Publishers Ltd
108 Cowley Road
Oxford OX4 1JF
UK

Blackwell Publishers Inc.
350 Main Street
Malden, Massachusetts 02148
USA

British Library Cataloguing in Publication Data

A CIP catalogue record for this book is available from the British Library.

Library of Congress Cataloging-in-Publication Data has been applied for.

ISBN 0–631–21832–7   (hbk)
ISBN 1–55786–849–2   (pbk)

Typeset in 10½ on 13pt Baskerville
by Graphicraft Limited, Hong Kong
Printed in Great Britain by TJ International, Padstow, Cornwall

This book is printed on acid-free paper.

Contents

This book is a collection of cases and projects in the area of international management. The cases and projects focus on cultural issues and show how culture influences behavior in the workplace. Members of different societies apply different cultural values when they make and implement decisions. An individual's national culture influences how the manager deals with other people in superior–subordinate, peer, buyer–seller, negotiation and consultancy relationships. In all these relationships, three questions arise:

- when are cultural factors a significant influence?
- when are other factors of greater influence?
- how can the importance of these different factors be weighed?

National culture also influences organizational culture. In the case of a foreign subsidiary, their national culture influences how members interpret the priorities set by headquarters. This means that headquarters cannot assume that headquarters' strategies and regulations are implemented in the same way by different subsidiaries when these belong in different national cultural contexts. The cases and projects in this book deal with all these issues.

This collection can be used to support a textbook by the same author, *International Management: Cross-Cultural Dimensions* (1998, second edition, Blackwell Publishers). But use of the textbook is not essential, and the collection is designed so that it can be used on its own.

Who Is The Book For?

The book has been written for students from MBA, other graduate management and some undergraduate programs. It is recommended for students majoring in international management with a focus on cultural factors. Many students who use this book may be non-native speakers of English.

The development of international business means that today's management student is almost certain to work with members of other cultures during his or her career. This may mean working at a multinational headquarters or on attachment to an operation abroad, whether on long expatriate appointments or short consultancies. The cases and projects in this collection aim to develop the cross-cultural skills that the modern manager needs.

What Makes This Book Different?

The cases are short, and are intended to illustrate issues that typically arise in international management classes. They can be prepared as homework assignments and discussed in class.

The cases are based on actual events, although all company names have been changed and all characters are fictitious (other than those quoted from newspaper and journal sources). There are three reasons for this fictionalization. Because the cases are intended for completion within a single classroom session, the real episodes have needed to be simplified and quantitative data have been excluded. Secondly, the writer believes that students find it easier to work on self-contained problems than with the problems facing real-life organizations about which they may have insider knowledge – which, in practice, can distort rather than illuminate classroom analysis. Thirdly, the material is intended for use by students from different cultural backgrounds, and the use of data from overtly real-life organizations can intimidate those who need organizational history explained to them.

The book is divided into two parts: Cases and Projects. In Part I – Cases – each case is prefaced by Case Preparation material. This introduces the area of interest and aims to spark class discussion. The Questions following the main material give practice in case analysis. The Decision questions ask how the analysis can be applied in practice. These two short sections also develop two essential business skills: writing problem-solution treatments and giving presentations.

Part II – Projects – aims to motivate by engaging students in real-life activities. Some of the projects call for research that can be conducted within the students' domain of shared professional experience, the business school. The projects set out here in this book encourage decisions and applications that may have clear relevance to this situation.

ACKNOWLEDGMENTS

A number of people have assisted this project. Useful suggestions and encouragement have come from a range of sources. I am particularly grateful to students who worked with earlier drafts of the material, in particular to students in the MBA program, SasinGIBA (Chulalongkorn University, Thailand), the MA: Business World programs of the School for Oriental and African Studies (the University of London), and the International Foundation Course for Overseas Students programs, also of SOAS. Draft material was read by a SOAS colleague, Keith Jackson.

I must express my continued appreciation of the enthusiasm and patient support given me by all Blackwell staff, and in particular by Catriona King and Bridget Jennings.

Finally, I wish to thank Blackwell Publishers for permission to reproduce material from *International Management*, second edition, and from its accompanying Instructor's Manual.

Dr Richard Mead
Director of Asian Business Studies
The School of Oriental and African Studies
The University of London

part

I

cases

case

introduction to culture

Albert had always enjoyed adventure. He lived his early years in the Austrian Tyrol but by the time he graduated from the local college he had grown bored of the comforts and complacencies of small-town life. He shocked his parents by announcing his plan to spend the next twenty years travelling outside Europe. Two weeks later he boarded a flight to Nairobi.

In Kenya he worked as a hotel barman, then moved to South Africa and managed a car rental business. Several other jobs followed, managing a range of enterprises. He moved to Latin America and started teaching in Brazil, and to his surprise discovered that he enjoyed the work and had a natural talent. In the early 1990s he arrived in Indonesia and took an MBA course taught at distance by a British business school. He started teaching first degree management studies at a university and after two years was promoted to managing the prestigious MBA program, organized under the auspices of an American partner, the Nettleton School.

Early in his travels he had realized how much he could learn by observing people at work. How people from the same culture behaved in the workplace taught valuable lessons about the values that they might take for granted. Educational institutions were no exception. Although students, administrators and teachers from the same culture might belong to different age and socioeconomic groups and have different goals in working together, they often accepted the same priorities in relating to each other.

In the Jakarta business school, Albert was interested by the loyalties shown by students in friendship circles. Teaching in some subjects was conducted in small study groups, and this might mean breaking up a friendship circle between groups. In theory, all groups ended at twelve noon for a one-hour lunch break. But usually, some groups were late breaking up. Typically, friends would wait for all members of their circle to collect from their different groups before they went to eat together.

A number of Americans had cross-registered from Nettleton for a few courses and noticed the same behavior. Brad approached Albert.

"Why do they wait so long?" he asked.

"We'll ask them in class," Albert promised.

At first the Indonesians were silent, even puzzled. They took their behavior for granted as the correct way to behave with friends.

"How long would you wait?" Brad asked.

"You know when classes end. Usually not so long," said Aziz.

"Yes, but how long would you wait for, say Sanyoto here, if his professor held him back?"

"As long as it would take. Twenty minutes, longer."

"That's the way we should behave."

"But not so long that we don't have time for lunch ourselves," said Junus, and all laughed.

The Americans were aghast.

"Why? You can meet him later in the day."

"Because he'd feel put down. If we don't wait, he must think we don't want his friendship."

"What we can't understand," said Sanyoto, "is why you Americans never wait at all."

"Yes," said Albert. "Brad, how long would you stand around if George here was held back?"

"No more than two minutes," said Brad.

"And for Brad, not at all," joked George.

"Then what?"

"I'd go for lunch."

"Even if it meant eating on your own?" asked Ali, shocked.

"Of course. I have to prepare to read, write term papers, prepare for study group meetings."

There was an embarrassed silence. The force of George's comment was clear to all. The Americans had complained before that when their study groups met, their Indonesian colleagues spent too much time in social chat and that progress often moved at the pace of the least-prepared one present.

"We think your two minutes only is very cold, unfriendly," said Ali.

"Your twenty minutes wait does not make efficient use of time," said Stuart.

"And you not waiting for Brad? How do you think he feels? Sad and alone. Is that efficient? Can he work with you again?"

"Of course he can. He wouldn't behave any differently with me."

"If my friends came out of class and discovered I had waited twenty minutes, they would think I was . . . very odd," Greg said, and that released the tension.

"That was interesting," said Albert. "But now decide. Is either side correct? And if not, how do we explain the difference?"

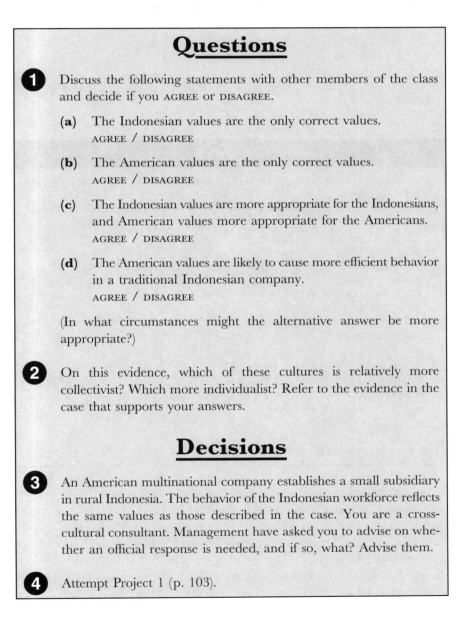

Questions

1 Discuss the following statements with other members of the class and decide if you AGREE or DISAGREE.

(a) The Indonesian values are the only correct values.
AGREE / DISAGREE

(b) The American values are the only correct values.
AGREE / DISAGREE

(c) The Indonesian values are more appropriate for the Indonesians, and American values more appropriate for the Americans.
AGREE / DISAGREE

(d) The American values are likely to cause more efficient behavior in a traditional Indonesian company.
AGREE / DISAGREE

(In what circumstances might the alternative answer be more appropriate?)

2 On this evidence, which of these cultures is relatively more collectivist? Which more individualist? Refer to the evidence in the case that supports your answers.

Decisions

3 An American multinational company establishes a small subsidiary in rural Indonesia. The behavior of the Indonesian workforce reflects the same values as those described in the case. You are a cross-cultural consultant. Management have asked you to advise on whether an official response is needed, and if so, what? Advise them.

4 Attempt Project 1 (p. 103).

case

2

the professor's shoes

CASE PREPARATION

Your company has decided to post you to manage a subsidiary in a country that you know nothing about.

How do you learn about the new culture? List the ADVANTAGES and DISADVANTAGES of each of the following:

Before you arrive,
- read guide books.
- ask repatriates.
- attend classes on the culture.
- (any other . . .)

After you arrive,
- observe.
- ask insiders (members of the culture).
- ask outsiders (expatriates).
- read newspapers.
- attend classes on the culture.
- (any other . . .)

Discuss your answers with the class.

Jack was a Professor in an Australian university. He taught engineering in a small but prestigious College of Mining. The College had signed a teaching and consultancy contract with a Thai engineering school. A number of the faculty had already been over to Thailand to teach a six-week course in their specialty, and now it was Jack's turn.

He was feeling both excited and apprehensive when the plane landed at Bangkok International Airport. He knew very little about Thai culture. Colleagues had told him that the Thais were a hospitable people, who valued good manners. They had given him a list of restaurants and night spots. He was determined to be a good guest and to fit into the culture as well as he was able.

He caught the connecting flight on to the provincial town where the school was situated.

He was met there by the school secretary, who drove him to the hotel where the school lodged its visitors. On the way he asked, "What should I know about Thai culture?"

She laughed, and after a moment's thought said, "Always take off your shoes when you enter important places."

Jack had heard of nothing like this before and he asked for confirmation. "You take your shoes off in all important places?"

"That's right. To show respect."

That first evening he went out by himself to eat dinner, and then went on to a bar. The free and easy nature of Thai night life delighted him, and he felt immediately at home. "There are no rules here," he told himself. "Anything goes."

On his first day of classes, Jack took off his shoes before entering the classroom and left them outside. He was mildly surprised to notice that the thirty students had all kept their shoes on. Because he was determined not to say anything that might be interpreted as bad manners, he decided to say nothing about it.

On the second day also, he left his shoes outside the classroom and taught in his socks. The same thing happened on the third, and succeeding days.

The students were mid-level professionals, with some experience of the world, and were initially amused. But as the situation continued, their amusement turned to irritation. Most irritated was one of the few foreign students in the class, another Australian, Kyle, who was being made to feel defensive of his nationality by his colleagues' comments.

Kyle eventually decided to talk with an English-language teacher working in the school. Peter had come to Thailand as a volunteer eight years before, liked the country, and decided to stay.

"The students don't like the professor taking his shoes off before he comes into the classroom."

"Is that what he does?"

"Yes. So please, could you suggest that he keeps them on?"

"Why don't you tell him yourself?"

"Because I have to get a good grade on his course. If he thinks I've embarrassed him, he's going to pick me off. So please, keep my name out of it."

So the next day, Peter went to talk to Jack in his office. Jack had just come out of teaching material that hadn't been as successful as he had expected, and he was not in the best of moods.

"Professor, can I talk to you a minute?" Peter asked.

"Sure, but only for a minute."

"How are you enjoying the assignment?"

"Fine. Is that it?"

"No. The students wonder if you could keep your shoes on in the classroom."

"When I need the advice of a volunteer, I'll ask for it," said Jack, who was in no mood to defend himself.

"But the students asked me to talk to you . . ."

"How many?"

"One."

"That's not a majority."

"It was a delegation. He was speaking on behalf of the full class. That's the Thai way."

"Then I'll hold a vote in class. If a majority vote for me to keep my shoes on, I will. That's democratic."

"It's not in Thai culture to take an open vote like that."

"Why not?"

"Because no one would want you to lose face by voting against you."

"Why not?"

"Because you're the social superior."

"When a majority of the class come and see me, I'll think about it. I was told to take off my shoes in important places, to show respect. And as a teacher, I think the classroom is a very important place that I want to respect – even if the students don't."

"No, important places are temples, houses, places like that . . ."

"And for me, the classroom."

Peter reported this conversation back to Kyle, who summarized it for his colleagues.

Jack did not change his behavior. The students were too shy to approach such an important person directly. Instead, they made a formal complaint to the school principal.

Jack enjoyed his visit. On the morning of his departure he paid a courtesy visit to the principal, and the principal said how grateful they were for his participation in the program. On the basis of these kind words, Jack returned home certain that he would be invited to return the following year. But the invitation never came.

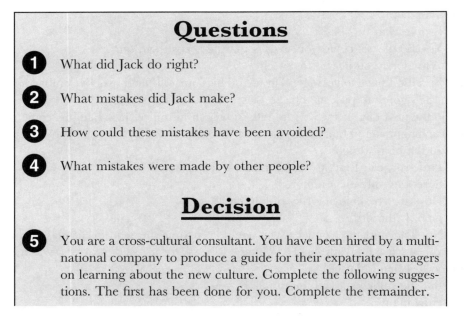

Questions

1 What did Jack do right?

2 What mistakes did Jack make?

3 How could these mistakes have been avoided?

4 What mistakes were made by other people?

Decision

5 You are a cross-cultural consultant. You have been hired by a multinational company to produce a guide for their expatriate managers on learning about the new culture. Complete the following suggestions. The first has been done for you. Complete the remainder.

DO ask insiders about the norms of their culture.

DO ....

DO ....

DO ....

DO ....

DON'T ....

DON'T ....

DON'T ....

DON'T ....

the New Delhi Tea Company

CASE PREPARATION

With which of these three statements do you agree?

A The first responsibility of the CEO is to protect the interests of his employees, even when this means giving up a business opportunity.

B The first responsibility of the CEO is to take up every possible business opportunity, even when this means damaging the interests of his employees.

C The statements in A: and B: above are false. The interests of the employees are best served by taking up every business opportunity available. Situations in which company business does NOT serve the interests of the employees never occur.

Discuss your answer with other members of the class. Try to reach agreement.

The New Delhi Tea Company was established in 1946 by Mr Gupta Shahani's elder brother, B.J. Shahani. The core business had consisted of purchasing tea from plantations and exporting to Europe and then Australia. In 1948, Gupta joined his sibling as the junior partner.

Demand fluctuated but most years saw increased profits. Business grew. Increasing numbers of persons from outside the family were hired in labouring and secretarial capacities. B.J. and Gupta began to consider the options for expanding their management capacity. B.J.'s unmarried daughter, Jamilla, was a Cambridge-trained accountant, and they invited her to join them. This was considered innovatory in an age when few middle-class Indian women worked outside the house, but the brothers had no doubts about her ability.

Gupta and his wife had no children, and as the need for management talent grew more acute, it was decided to approach their two cousins, the sons of their uncle. Sanjiv and K.L. had business experience, and at that time worked in a British-owned multinational in middle management posts. They were keen to join, but B.J. and Gupta disagreed about what value they could bring to the firm.

"It's most important we keep the business in the family. We can't afford to have outsiders pushing their noses into everything," said B.J.

"But Sanjiv and K.L. . . .," Gupta began tentatively.

"I know. They aren't the brightest members of the family."

"We must modernize, even if that means hiring from outside. The way the world is changing now we have independence from the British, we can't afford to be left behind. We need new technology, new ideas, and people who know how to use them."

B.J. persisted. "They don't have your business imagination. But they're both determined, if a little slow, and committed to the family. Money can't buy loyalty. And both are family men. They have sons." Sanjiv had two sons and two daughters, and K.L. had produced Zubin and another child was on the way.

"Let's hope they're more intelligent than their parents," Gupta had concluded.

That was the last time the brothers talked. B.J. looked at his watch and announced that he and Jamilla – who had accompanied her father – would drive home.

"It's too late," Gupta said. "You're exhausted. You can phone Fauzia (B.J.'s wife) and tell her that you're both staying here."

"Nonsense dear brother, thank you but ten minutes drive isn't too far at any time. And Jamilla has an early appointment tomorrow."

The street lights that night were flickering worse than usual. In the shadows, B.J. had swerved to avoid a cow grazing on a corner of Penlochrie Road, and ploughed into a stone wall. Death was instantaneous. Jamilla never fully recovered from her injuries. An invalid, she was forced to retire from an active management role – although she continued to spend weekends scrutinizing the books and querying every detail that worried her acute intelligence.

Feeling remorseful, Gupta quickly invited his cousins to join the firm, Sanjiv as finance manager and K.L. as marketing manager. He made clear that their sons would also be welcomed when they had completed their educations.

By 1988, Ram, Rashid, Zubin and his younger brother Pradeep had all joined the firm in managerial positions. Pradeep had grauated two years before with a top MBA from the London Business School.

Figure 3.1 shows the company structure at this point. Only those members with an interest in managing the family business are included. (Jamilla's informal participation is not indicated.)

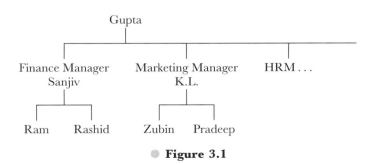

● **Figure 3.1**

By the late 1980s the tea business had expanded to the point that the firm was suffering acute warehousing problems. After some thought Gupta sent Ram to study management information systems in the United States.

"Find us a computer warehousing system that can solve the needs of a small business like ours", he asked. When Ram reported that the market offered nothing that precisely meeted their needs.

"Then you design one yourself."

Ram enrolled in a new course that taught him all he needed to know about program design, and he wrote a specialized package. The family experimented; it precisely matched their needs.

The news of this success leaked out and several other small businesses enquired where they might purchase the package. After some thought, Gupta asked Ram – now Production Manager – to take a course on software production. He then established a new company. The family agreed that Ram should delegate some of his responsibilities in the flagship company and take on the new venture as Managing Director.

NDT Software was soon profitable. By 1993 Gupta was wondering how to develop the firm when an acquaintance suggested assembling computers. The family entered an agreement with a Taiwanese company to assemble their low-priced range for the sub-continental market. The fledgling company, NDT Assembly, was placed under the direction of Rashid. By this stage, the New Delhi Tea Company, NDT Software and NDT Assembly were employing a total of over a thousand people.

The structure of the New Delhi Tea Company and the conglomerate at this point is represented by figures 3.2 and 3.3, which shown the formal participation of family members.

THE NEW DELHI TEA COMPANY: President/MD; Gupta

Finance Manager Sanjiv	Marketing Manager K.L.	Production Manager Ram	Engineering Manager Rashid	HR Manager Zubin	R&D Manager Pradeep

Figure 3.2

THE NEW DELHI TEA COMPANY

President/MD: Gupta

NDT SOFTWARE: President;   Gupta
                MD;   Ram

NDT ASSEMBLY: President;   Gupta
                MD;   Rashid

Figure 3.3

One day, Pradeep approached Gupta and said, "Uncle, I have been wondering." He hesitated respectfully, then when the old man gave his attention, continued. "Why do we stop at assembling for some other company? We have the experience to start manufacturing under our own label."

"And the markets?" By this stage the office computer market was already crowded.

"We specialize on computational equipment for hospitals. As the professional middle class grow wealthier they invest more in their health. For instance, at present all scanning and ECT plant is imported."

Gupta looked through the summary business plan that the young man had written and concluded "We need an international partner." He smiled. "And you have thought of that too."

"Yes uncle", said Pradeep. "You may remember that when I was doing the MBA, I shared a house with a good friend, Peter. He once visited us in the vacation. Now he is working for a prominent medical equipment firm, Norttel-medic. They are planning to expand into India and are looking for a joint-venture partner."

"Why should they want to work with us?"

"Of course, there are many other firms that are looking for this opportunity." Pradeep listed five of their competitors of which at least two, Zadiv Electronics and Hasan Brothers boasted deeper technological bases. "But Peter at least is convinced that we have a management style that complements theirs."

The family met over a weekend and agreed to negotiate. Thanks to Pradeep's connections, discussions proceeded quickly. Groups of managers from each company visited the other. Gupta's family became increasingly excited about the proposal, which offered the family business unusual opportunities to secure technology transfer and to develop an international reputation. Even Jamilla, who had treated every previous development with the deepest scepticism expressed her enthusiasm. Then the CEO of Norttel-medic visited for a confidential meeting with Gupta.

Bob Robinson came quickly to the point. "Our people have had useful discussions and we're happy to cooperate on a joint venture company, say NDT–Nortell – assuming we settle on the details." He reviewed the financial plan, production standards and quality control, marketing policy, human resource policy, proposals for technology transfer and its implications for the human resource policy. None of these posed any serious difficulties. "But we do have one problem. And that's why I suggested we meet alone. Frankly, we are not happy with your senior managers."

"My family."

"Yes, we appreciate that this gives you a problem. But while they may be entirely competent to manage a local operation, they don't have the experience and breadth for an international project like this." He summarized his team's assessments of Ram, Sanjiv, K.L., Ram, Rashid and Zubin. Gupta tried to defend his team, but was forced to admit to himself that many of the criticisms were apt.

"We're sorry that Miss Jamilla is not able to participate. We have been most impressed by her comments. That leaves your cousin Pradeep."

Bob spelled out his terms. Norttel-medic would be happy to form a project with NDT on condition that the project was managed by Pradeep. "He has a very good MBA qualification. He has shown the entrepreneurial flair and imagination that we need. We have observed him closely and are confident that he has the right management skills. If that is not acceptable to you, we will be forced to open discussions with one of your competitors."

Gupta did not enjoy passing on this decision to his senior management team. Neither Sanjiv nor K.L. wanted the responsibility of managing the previous projects, but this had far greater status, and each felt himself qualified. Sanjiv said "What Bob proposes is a slap in the face. He is insulting the family. Yes, Pradeep is clever, but he is still young. If he is given this post, he will think that he is the most important person in the family. More important than his elder brother and cousins and uncle, even more important than his own father." And although K.L. was proud of his gifted son, even he seemed unwilling to accept the risk.

Gupta felt that the two were already preparing a compromise by which Ram's name would go forward on condition that Zubin took over Ram's Managing Directorship in MDT Software. But he knew that Bob would not accept anyone other than Pradeep to run the new venture.

"An opportunity like this will not return," he sighed. Now he had to decide whether to allow Pradeep's appointment and thus sacrifice unity in the family, or to tell Bob that he could not accept his terms.

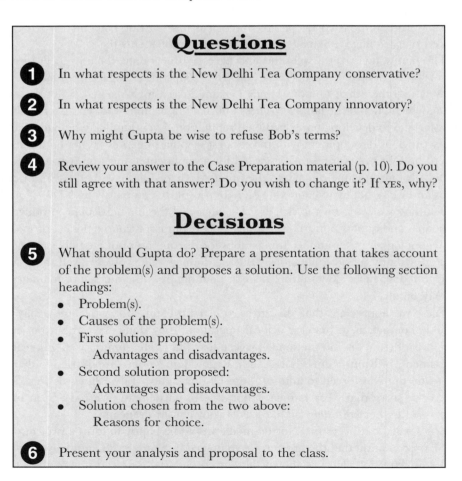

Questions

1 In what respects is the New Delhi Tea Company conservative?

2 In what respects is the New Delhi Tea Company innovatory?

3 Why might Gupta be wise to refuse Bob's terms?

4 Review your answer to the Case Preparation material (p. 10). Do you still agree with that answer? Do you wish to change it? If YES, why?

Decisions

5 What should Gupta do? Prepare a presentation that takes account of the problem(s) and proposes a solution. Use the following section headings:
  - Problem(s).
  - Causes of the problem(s).
  - First solution proposed:
      Advantages and disadvantages.
  - Second solution proposed:
      Advantages and disadvantages.
  - Solution chosen from the two above:
      Reasons for choice.

6 Present your analysis and proposal to the class.

how much structure?

CASE PREPARATION

With which of these two statements do you agree most strongly?

   A   In general, every company benefits from a HIGH degree of formal structuring and bureaucratic control.

   B   In general, every company benefits from a LOW degree of formal structuring and bureaucratic control.

Discuss your answer with other members of the class. If your opinions differ, how do you explain the difference? How do you explain different opinions held by members of different cultures represented in the class?

Read the following two case histories before attempting the Questions and Decisions at the end of Case 4.

1   The Furniture Company

In 1997 the Mexican economy was booming. Two Mexican entrepreneurs, Mario Angelico and Franz Camozetti, sat down to analyse the spiralling demand for office accommodation. They realized that the demand for office furniture was also certain to grow, and offered tremendous opportunities for investment. They formed a five-year joint venture with a Finnish furniture company. The new venture, MariFFin, had the goal of importing cheap furniture in kit form, assembling, then distributing throughout the country and region.

The venture was an immediate success. Within four months the number of employees had risen from four to 28, but the organization was largely unstructured. Recognizing the need for bureaucratic controls, Mario and Franz called a meeting of their departmental managers. Within twenty minutes a structure was agreed. There would be five departments; Sales, Production, Importing, Finance and Administration. Brief job descriptions were written for the managers and their assistants.

Helmut Borges, the Production manager, had arrived at the meeting late. He was still examining the diagram sketched on the board as the entrepreneurs rushed out of the room. "Where's the warehousing unit in this structure?"

"Under sales," said the Sales manager.

"Under importing," said the Import manager.

"Production," said Helmut.

"We'd better check," said the Administration manager. But by then it was too late. As they looked out of the window, Mario and Franz disappeared into a hired car.

"Where are they going?"

"The airport," explained Fiamma Pizzaconi, the secretary. "They have a meeting in São Paulo with a possible customer."

A day later, Fiamma circulated a memo. A warehousing head (to be appointed) would report to the Import manager.

"That can't work," said Helmut.

Fiamma shrugged. "Tell the partners."

"Where are they today?"

"Costa Rica."

Two years later the pay roll had risen to 380 persons. The basic structure had not changed, although a number of sub-units had been formed. For instance, a human resources unit was developed within the Administration department. Mario and Franz refused to delegate authority for taking policy decisions, and because the company was still performing successfully none of their employees felt inclined to disagree.

The effects of growth and with the changing business environment began to strain the structure to its limits. The company's cheaper brands were increasingly challenged both by local competitors and by imports from less-developed countries in the region. The partners responded by dropping their cheaper lines and planning a new line of executive furniture. Previously the few needs for marketing had been contracted to a consultancy, but now the need for in-house market research was obvious. In addition, the sales department needed more sophisticated skills in order to penetrate the new market, and this meant that training was needed. But who should provide that training?

The new head of Human Resources, Enrico Glass, insisted that his department should be responsible for all in-house training. Hugo Smythe of Sales responded that he be given the resources to establish his own training unit.

Glass:	"The company cannot afford to make that investment for one department only."
Smythe:	"No. The company is going to need high-level sales training on a continuing basis."
Glass:	"All training should be concentrated in one department – which is my department."
Smythe:	"You cannot understand the needs of a modern sales department. The human resource function should be restricted to recruitments, appraisals, employment contracts, that sort of thing. My managers understand our training needs and you don't."

Glass: "If you think that, lend us one of your managers to work with my people on designing the training syllabus and materials."

Smythe: "My people are too busy. I cannot afford to post them around the company to help out those departments that don't know their own business. And let's be clear about one thing. Your unit still reports to Administration. You do not have the status of a full department."

Glass: "That is not the point. Training is my business. My unit was established with absolute control over all training in the company."

Smythe: "I have seen nothing on paper that says so."

Glass: "Mario and Franz promised me that when they hired me."

The other managers listened uneasily. Some favored the idea of centralizing all training. They wanted to avoid the expense of duplicating training support services in all departments.

Others preferred to keep training on a departmental basis. Helmut had already devoted resources to planning a short training programme for his new lathe operators. He had never been informed that Human Resources claimed responsibility for this function.

"The issue is this," he said. "We have problems of internal communication. The partners are going to have to decide. Where are they this week?"

"Moscow," snapped Fiamma.

"Doing a deal," said Enrico.

"Don't blame me." Fiamma was fed up with having to explain why Mario and Franz were never on the premises. "But they return on Tuesday."

"Then book them for a meeting on Tuesday."

"Can't. They're meeting all day. And on Wednesday Mario flies to Geneva."

"What about Franz?"

"Hong Kong."

Helmut groaned. "I'm taking on another four carpenters and five mechanics next week. We must get this resolved as soon as possible."

Fiamma asked "Get what resolved?"

2 The Teng Family Company Invest in the MBA

In Kaohsiung, Taiwan, the Teng family owned a profitable drygoods store. In the early years of their marriage, both Mr and Mrs Teng had worked hard to make the shop a success. Then the children came.

By the time he was eleven, the eldest son Bruce was already used to working there. In school holidays, at weekends and when he had completed his study assignments in the evening, the boy swept the floors of the dusty old building, stocked shelves, and began serving customers. He was followed by a brother Weiming, sister Ya-yuan, then brothers Xia-ming and Joseph, who was the youngest by five years. The business prospered, and the family moved to a modern shop a few blocks from the town centre.

When the children left school, they begun working full time. Mrs Teng still occupied the shop from early working to evening. She spent her time behind the cash register, fixing her sharp eyes on her children and the manual labourers, and haranguing them in raucous terms whenever they seemed to be about to drop something or fail to stack the goods correctly or to make some other mistake.

The labourers were not family members and never chose to stay long – even those that survived the threat of dismissal in the first few days. The children argued among themselves how long this one or that one might last, and were always secretly delighted to hear their fierce Mother send another one away.

Mr Teng spent more and more of his time at the Happy Paradise Gun and Social Club, which had elected him to an important post. He said that he found it quieter than life in the shop.

Then one day, a friend mentioned that representatives of a Swedish motor manufacturer, Swedsa, were in town looking for an established and respectable business that could act as a local dealer. He went home to discuss the matter with his family, and the next morning he and Bruce approached the Swedes in their hotel. Within several meetings and a few weeks later, the papers were prepared and the Teng family business was accredited as official dealer of Swedsa products in the south of Taiwan.

This happened during the early years of the 1990s. In the first years, growth was rapid. A showroom, office block and engineering workshops were soon erected. Mr Teng was officially President but had taken over management of the drygoods store and between that and the club was seldom seen. Mrs Teng now ran the auto dealership. A nephew Peter and his wife joined Mr Teng. Peter had trained as a Jaguar salesman and demonstrated energy and talent. The four eldest Teng children were now exclusively occupied in the new business.

There was no formal structuring. As was typical of a Taiwanese family business, Mrs Teng controlled the finances. Otherwise, nobody had a formal job title or was tied to a single area of responsibilities. Bruce spoke the best English and usually dealt with Swedish headquarters, but he also enjoyed engineering, which he shared with Wei-ming who also marketed the family products. Ya-yuan worked closely with her mother in employing and managing the non-family staff.

The extrovert Xia-ming had developed a taste for motor-racing and acquired a circle of wealthy friends who would visit him in the showroom and expect to take the latest model for a test-drive. He took some of the responsibilities for sales, but left the clerical aspects of the job to his new fiancee, Joanne.

Joanne, who had recently returned from high school and junior college in California, had favorably impressed them all. She was hard working and appeared entirely loyal to the family company. Soon she was adding to her work load by helping Ya-yuan in administration, so Ya-yuan was free to assist her mother by keeping the accounts. She enrolled for an accounting course at the local technical college.

The lack of structure posed no difficulties for the Swedes once they had realized that all communications should be directed through Bruce. On the rare occasions that Bruce was absent or indisposed, they could expect to deal with Ya-yuan.

At this point Wei-ming spent a year in Australia taking an MBA degree. He was the quietest of the children but the best student, and had taught himself the principles of marketing when still at school. During this year Joseph completed his training as a mechanic and took his place.

When Wei-ming returned with his new qualification he asked to examine the books. Two days later he confronted the family at dinner. "We give too much credit," he said. "We shouldn't let our customers take ownership of our products before they pay more on account. Our debt ratios are not competitive." He explained, "we owe too much to the bank."

Mr Teng explained, "We have to give our customers very easy terms. We treat them like our friends. That's the way to keep them coming back."

Wei-ming protested, "But technically, we're bankrupt."

They all laughed.

"Of course we're not," his Mother told him. "You're forgetting, this is Taiwan. We give our friends credit, they give us credit. Your MBA school told you that all business agreements must be written down. But that does not always happen in Taiwan. We trust our friends."

Wei-min was embarrassed. After a few minutes he said, "There's one thing we can use, though. To be efficient we need more organization. We need a structure." He spelled out the details. "For example, it's no good Xia-ming managing the showroom and sales and sometimes engineering. We need to know everybody's responsibilities and where everybody is at any time."

Ya-yuan said, "But there's only us, Joanne, old Mr Chien and Mrs Oi, and the showroom staff and the casuals. Thats us and another eleven people. And the buildings aren't that big, we always know where to find each other."

"Yes, but what about the future? If we are going to grow we need better organization to cope with it."

However, the idea appealed to them. After some thought and further discussion they agreed on a company structure and specified their different areas of responsibility in a formal policy document. The motor company management structure is set out in figure 4.1. Mrs Teng held control of day-to-day management and the financial function. The five children were made responsible for the other main functions. As head of administration Joanne reported directly to Mrs Teng, but did not have management status.

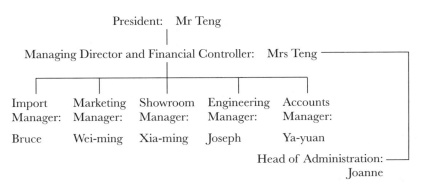

● **Figure 4.1**

At first, they found it difficult to adapt to their new roles. Xia-ming could not break his habit of taking visitors into the engineering workshop and tinkering with the engines, which annoyed Joseph. He also argued with Wei-ming over which jobs should belong to the marketing function and which to sales in the showroom. Supposing that a customer visited the showroom and asked to be sent details of all new models in the coming year, who should be responsible?

"His first contact is the showroom so he's my customer," said Xia-ming.

"But he's not interested in the current models, he's asking about the future. That's a marketing question, he's my customer."

"Ridiculous," said Ya-yuan.

In time though, they learnt to restrict themselves to their formal roles. They wanted to avoid the angry scenes that had broken out when the structures were first introduced. But still, the promised growth did not come. They had taken on only one more staff member. By 1996 profits had levelled out. There was no obvious reason. The economy was still booming and their neighbours reported an excellent year.

Ya-yuan asked her eldest brother, "Do you remember when that foreigner came in wanting to hire? And you said that we don't do hirings? So he went to the Golden Apple showroom. They gave him the service he wanted – Cecelia Lim told me herself."

"We made a rule against hiring," Bruce replied. "If I had broken the rule for that one customer, Wei-ming would still be complaining."

She reminded him of further occasions when opportunities were overlooked. "There was the time you closed at seven although we knew that the fleet manager from the Kaohsiung Dragon hotel wanted to visit and had been delayed."

"We always close at seven."

"And when you and Mother decided that only administrative staff should move the furniture into the new offices. We had to close for two hours. Who knows what business we lost?"

"Everybody has his own job – or her own job."

"In the old days it didn't matter. Everybody did what they could to help the family."

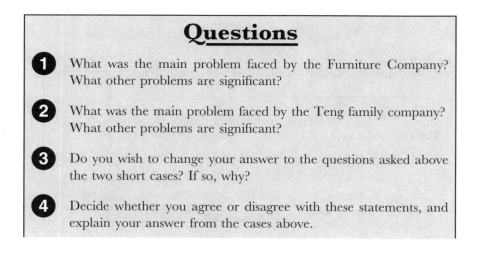

Questions

1 What was the main problem faced by the Furniture Company? What other problems are significant?

2 What was the main problem faced by the Teng family company? What other problems are significant?

3 Do you wish to change your answer to the questions asked above the two short cases? If so, why?

4 Decide whether you agree or disagree with these statements, and explain your answer from the cases above.

(a) Every company needs a high degree of bureaucratic organization; the more the better.
AGREE (if so, why?) / DISAGREE (if so, why?)

(b) In every company, the right level of bureaucratic organization is determined by the ownership structure.
AGREE (if so, why?) / DISAGREE (if so, why?)

(c) In every company, the right level of bureaucratic organization is determined by the size of the workforce.
AGREE (if so, why?) / DISAGREE (if so, why?)

(d) In every company, the right level of bureaucratic organization is determined by the customer base.
AGREE (if so, why?) / DISAGREE (if so, why?)

(e) In every company, the right level of bureaucratic organization is determined by factors associated with the industry in which it competes.
AGREE (if so, why?) / DISAGREE (if so, why?)

(f) Every company should avoid bureaucratic organization; the less the better.
AGREE (if so, why?) / DISAGREE (if so, why?)

5 If you DISAGREE with ALL the statements in 1a–1f above, complete the statement below, and explain your suggestion.

In every company, the right level of bureaucratic organization is

determined by ....

....

Because ....

....

6 Do you think that a company with a strong entrepreneurial culture faces particular management problems in designing and operating an effective structure?

If YES, what problems?

7 Do you think that a family company faces particular management problems in designing and operating an effective structure?

If YES, what problems?

Decisions

8 You are a consultant. You have been hired to analyse the problem(s) faced by the Furniture Company, and to propose a solution. Applying your answers above, use the following section headings:

- Problem(s).
- Causes of the problem(s).
- First solution proposed:
    Advantages and disadvantages.
- Second solution proposed:
    Advantages and disadvantages.
- Chosen solution:
    Reasons for choice.

9 Similarly, you have been hired to analyse the problem(s) faced by the Teng family company, and to propose a solution. Use the same section headings:

- Problem(s).
- Causes of the problem(s).
- First solution proposed:
    Advantages and disadvantages.
- Second solution proposed:
    Advantages and disadvantages.
- Chosen solution:
    Reasons for choice.

10 Present your analysis and proposals to the class.

the Pascale Automobile Company

The Pascale Automobile Company (PAC) is based in Davoston, Illinois. Five years ago, PAC began exporting its small four-door hatchback "Nafala" to Ruritania, where it was assembled. The car had a displacement of 1600 cc. Its success was immediate; 5,400 were sold in the first year.

Ruritania is one of the poorest countries in East Africa, and the roads of even the capital city are pitted and broken. The north of the country is mountainous, and small towns are connected by narrow winding roads that in winter are often blocked by rock falls. You can drive from the mountains, through sparse farming land to a tropical beach, in a few hours. The sturdy and inexpensive "Nafala" was perfectly suited to this variable terrain.

PAC had not expected so great a success, and a series of meetings considered the strategic implications. Paulo Zanetti, the Marketing Manager, proposed an export drive throughout the region. "The Nafala is not technically sophisticated. Nobody pretends that it is. But it can be driven, and repaired, anywhere in Africa."

Mario Pascale, the Chairman, liked the idea. "But we can go further", he said. "We should do more than assemble. We can start manufacturing, and take control of the region. Our competitors will be left standing."

"Manufacturing in Ruritania?" queried his nephew Ricardo.

The old man took the point. Materials and skills were in short supply. They were unlikely to find factory space that matched their specifications. "I want an economic analysis of Ruritania and its neighbors."

Ruritania's western border abutted on Darana. Darana was the economic power house of the region. Western and East Asian manufacturing industries had been established there for several years. The urban work force was increasingly experienced, and the booming economy had grown a new middle class.

"Darana can supply the work force we need and the market. From there we can export throughout the region," decided Pascale. He tapped the map.

"There's a modern seaport, an international airport, we can ship bulk in and out. The road system is good, among the best in the continent. We'll build on a greenfield site if we can't find plant that meets our needs. I want a project team over there within the month. This is a priority."

A core project team met. Two sub-teams were made responsible, one for organizing the Daranese strategy and operations and the second for planning headquarters control systems in respect to the subsidiary. Negotiations with the Daranese government guaranteed PAC 90 percent ownership (a nominal 10 percent being held by a government body) in return for concessions of technology transfer and staff recruitment. Darana's investment, development and pay policies were generous. The immediate investment of $22 million would be doubled within four years. Production was set high; 10,000 units in the first year, rising 50,000 in five years. The plant was modern and pricing competitive.

PAC (Darana) was employing 550 persons in its first year, including 48 Daranese. Top management including all departmental managers were expatriated from headquarters, which also supplied some technical staff and senior supervisors. Daranese were appointed at assistant managerial levels in human resources, accounting and production departments, and to shadow assistant managers in all other departments. Technical development programmes were started to train Daranese supervisors and technicians.

The Daranese government allocated the PAC(D) expatriates homes on a compound reserved for American expatriates. This provided tight security and outsiders entered only with difficulty. In the early days, the PAC expatriates had arranged a social evening for their colleagues. But several local managers had been forced to spend an hour in the security guard house while their credentials were checked, and the evening had finished on a sour note. The experiment was not repeated.

PAC(D) expatriates lived comfortable lives. They limited their social lives to visiting with other PAC(D) employees and other Americans and Anglos, and meeting in the American social club. Their children went placed in an American school on the estate. For many, experience of Daranese life was limited to views through car windows as they went gliding along the well-kept highways to and from the plant every day, or waiting in lines of other luxury cars in the increasingly common traffic jams. A few had learned some words of Daranese before taking the posting, but their secretaries and immediate subordinates spoke good English and these modest language skills were seldom exercised. The more adventurous continued to experiment with Daranese food in some of the local restaurants.

Three years later, the project was facing serious difficulties. Sales had started healthily, then quickly peaked. No one could understand why. The economy was flourishing as never before, and the new class of young Daranese professionals were spending lavishly on symbols of their new status. They seemed to have money to spare. The sense of frustration within the company was hurting morale at all levels. Martin Toulsa, the chief executor, had heard stories of outsiders trying to organize an underground union and having some success.

One morning on the way to the plant, he was sitting brooding over these problems in the car. The Daranese managers were affected by this mood of pessimism. Many had been trained in top American and other business schools, and had joined with wide experience of the most successful companies in the Daranese private sector. Initially they had been optimistic and positive. But their morale had dropped. Increasingly they sent excuses for not attending meetings, and when they did come, were likely to sit in silence, avoiding eye contact with the expatriates.

Only the previous week, the assistant marketing manager had given notice to quit, on the ostensive grounds that his relatives wished him to join the family firm. Jatri had been flagged as a coming star and Martin was sorry to lose him. Further, he felt sure that Jatri had ideas of how to resolve the problems that faced the subsidiary, and would have been willing to air them in an informal setting away from their colleagues. But now the opportunity was lost.

Martin sat back and looked out at the streams of Japanese, German, and other European cars. He thought how the company was coming in for a lot of unfair criticism, fed by unfounded rumours from anonymous sources. A few days before the production manager, Chuck Connely, had come in waving a translation of an article in a local newspaper. "'Chronic management problems in PAC,'" he read. "Where do they get this stuff?" "'Local managers are confused about headquarters strategy.'" "That's nonsense. We tried explaining it but they won't listen." "'Marketing strategy has no direction.'" "Well, that's maybe."

Martin said nothing. Chuck's ongoing disagreements with the Marketing Department were well known. Martin wasn't about to make a comment that would be repeated outside his office and used to fan the flames of further discord. After a pause, Chuck went on. "And here. Fights in the canteen over inedible food. Have there been fights? Nobody told me."

Martin didn't know either.

"No, none of us has heard of any fights," the production manager concluded. "Lies. And they hurt us."

Questions

1 What factors internal to PAC(D) explain its failure?

2 What factors external to PAC(D) explain its failure?

Decisions

3 PAC headquarters is considering plans to establish subsidiaries elsewhere in Africa. You are a consultant and have been hired to advise on the opportunities and problems that might arise.

the European Union University Support Agency

CASE PREPARATION

A short time ago, a US report announced that the average executive receives about 90 messages or documents every day. These messages consist of phone calls, e-mail messages, voice mail messages, faxes, Post-It notes, phone message slips, inter-office/internal mail messages, paper messages, mail (traditional deliveries), cellular phone calls, overnight courier deliveries, express mail deliveries, local messenger deliveries.

Obviously, the executive cannot answer all these in the detail requested and still perform adequately.

How can the manager cope with this pressure effectively?

Discuss your answer with other members of the class.

The European Union University Support Agency (EUUSA) has the mission of providing information on the European Union to universities in non-European countries. It arranges conferences and academic publications devoted to EU topics and their applications to the local context. It covers the costs of travel and accommodation for visiting academics and faculty, and acts as a clearing agency for graduate students looking for scholarships and travel grants. EUUSA is represented widely in Asian countries which include Malaysia.

It is normal that expatriates occupy senior EUUSA posts at the ranks of Representative, Assistant Representative and Travel Officer. All others posts are taken by local nationals.

The Penang (Malaysia) Representative Office was headed by a Belgian, Louis Bossu, until last year when he took early retirement to live in Kelantan. This decision to stay in the country that he had grown to love was typical of Louis. He had always placed a priority on developing good personal relationships with those government officers and academics with whom he came into contact, and over 500 had attended his retirement party.

It had been Louis' routine to spend no more than two hours at his desk each day. In that time he made phone calls and reviewed ongoing operations with his Assistant Representative. He chatted to staff about their domestic lives. He delegated administrative activities whenever possible. The rest of the day was given up to receptions and official entertainment.

Over the many years of Louis' tenure, his easy-going work-style affected the organizational culture. Staff enjoyed the social aspects of their work but they grew casual in how they interpreted their job-descriptions. They avoided developing new initiatives that challenged their settled routines.

Staff were loyal to their local departmental heads, who made the routine decisions. The two strongest personalities were Mohamed Daouad, the Senior Librarian, and Abdul Haji Ibrahim, the Head of Finance. These two disliked each other and were frequently at loggerheads. When this happened, they called on the support of their factions and staff were used to dividing into two camps, usually over issues that were not important. When a storm blew up, Louis had kept out of the office altogether, sure that within a couple of days the appearance of peace would be restored.

Both the Assistant Representative, Burt Johansson, and the Travel Officer, Marie Penaars, had been posted here within the past year. Louis was replaced by an Irishman, John Fahey. John had originally trained as an accountant, and came with a reputation as a demanding manager. His appointment came at a time when Brussels headquarters was enforcing painful budget cutbacks.

All Representative offices were expected to give issues of financial accountability a high priority, and to set firm budgetry targets. It was important to maintain essential services, but to reduce unnecessary expenditures.

John spent the first week interviewing all staff, and then sat in their offices observing operations. He quickly realized that although staff enjoyed their jobs, discipline was lax. At the end of the week he briefed Burt and Marie, then called a general staff meeting. Departmental managers were asked to sit in a group apart from their subordinates.

"First, a list of questions. A number of points on which I am still unclear." He brought out a file of papers covered in his neat writing, and the managers shifted uncomfortably.

"Conference proposals. We seem to be using two different forms. Why?" After some muttered conversation someone explained the historical circumstances. The system had recently been revised in Brussels, and although most departments were using the revision, some were more comfortable with the original.

"That is not very satisfactory, is it? I hope that we can aim at uniformity."

It was pointed out that both forms derived the same information, but gave different emphases. These differences suited the needs of different departments.

"From now on we shall use only the up-to-date version. Next. We are using two commercial printers. Is that economical? And what can't we manage to print for ourselves?"

An hour later, he had moved on from procedure to discipline. He chose his words carefully. Several of the staff had made clear their affection for Louis, and he did not want to be seen to criticize the previous regime, whatever his personal feelings. He must not imply dishonesty on the part of any individual, or cause anyone to lose face.

"Mid-morning break is taking too long. Some people are extending the fifteen minute break to more than half an hour."

"No one is being criticized. I am sure that each of you has ideas of how to improve your own performance. I look forward to seeing these improvements." He made his final points. "I am hoping to work closely with your departmental managers. They know most about our organization and our work. So I'll be consulting them on all important matters. Talk to them. And please remember that you can always talk to me. My door is always open. If you have anything to add to what we have discussed, any ideas, do not hesitate to come and talk to me. Do not be afraid of disagreeing with me. I am always open to ideas, and if necessary I can change my mind. Thank you."

John watched them filing out silently. He knew from their expressions that they were not happy. But what else could he have said?

When they had separated into their regular lunchtime groups, their complaints were bitter.

"Louis never questioned how we contracted our caterers. In fact he always congratulated us on the makaan (food). And you can't always get the best service unless you pay the top price."

"We can't process the stationery invoices any faster than we do. Unless he wants to pay for overtime."

"Everybody knows that the European Union has plenty of money."

"Why can't we enjoy our morning break? Fifteen minutes isn't long enough, everybody knows that."

"And Louis drank his coffee with us."

John spent the next few weeks reviewing all procedures. He worked closely from the notes he had made in the general staff meeting. Disappointingly, nobody had come to his office in order to discuss any of the points raised in the meeting. He was pleased to note that the discipline problems were being resolved.

The next day the Deputy Librarian, Judy Shameri, waited patiently for twenty minutes outside his office while he completed a meeting with a visiting scholar. When he returned from escorting his visitor to the elevator, he noticed her. "Yes Judy?"

She showed him a copy of a journal on European financial policy. And explained, "Our subscription to EuroFinPol runs out next month. Should we renew it?"

John flipped through the closely-printed pages and asked, "What does Mohamed say?"

"He said to ask you. He said it's very expensive."

"Well, how many people use it? If it's popular then we should continue it. If not, let it drop."

Judy nodded thoughtfully and left.

John assumed that this problem was resolved. Then, a week later, Judy appeared again. She handed him a sheet of data. "We think that twenty-eight people read EuroFinPol this week," she said, "and seven for more than one hour."

He was astounded. "How did you find that out?"

"We watched them."

"But why?"

"Because you asked us to. And now we want to know if we must renew it or not."

"And what does Mr Mohamed think that we should do?"

"He thinks that we should ask you."

John shrugged helplessly. "What readership do our other journals attract? What is a typical figure?" Then, realizing how these questions might be interpreted he came to a decision. "Twenty-eight doesn't sound many to me. Cancel it."

This case was typical. The number of staff coming to his office to ask for advice on minor problems multiplied. Burt and Marie noticed the same tendency. Burt reported that he had been asked to check the menu for a buffet reception. "Ibrahim came to ask whether we should have chicken or shrimp. I asked him which was cheaper. He said chicken but most people prefer shrimp. I asked who are the guests. He said some important people, some not important. But we can't place notices on plates, for important guests, for unimportant guests. I told him some of both. That conversation took ten minutes. That costs my time."

A few days before he had been forced to cancel dinner out with his wife in order to decide on an order for new computers. He had come to the conclusion that the cheaper models would suit their needs. Then the Departmental Head had sent a memo explaining why the cheaper models would have to be replaced within eighteen months and were less economical. John had replied asking why that factor had not been taken into account when the original proposal was made. The Head responded that this was a decision for the Representative and not himself to make.

A few days later Mohamed Daouad appeared at his office.

"Professor Chen is waiting in my office."

John remembered a local academic whom he had recently met at a reception. "He is regular reader of the EuroFinPol. Now we have cancelled the subscription and he has come to complain. I am very sorry to say that your decision may not have been the best possible."

John went downstairs and spent twenty minutes calming the Professor, who seemed convinced that the European Union was downgrading its interests in the country. When he returned to his office he realized that he was now running late for a meeting with an important government official.

That evening John sat late in his office, feeling exhausted. He did not seem to have time to solve all the trivial problems that landed on his desk. How could he possibly catch up?

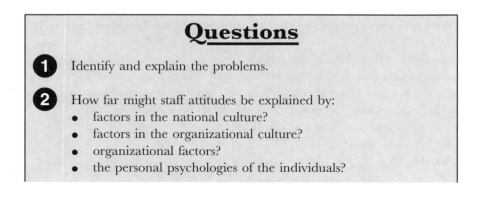

Questions

1 Identify and explain the problems.

2 How far might staff attitudes be explained by:
  - factors in the national culture?
  - factors in the organizational culture?
  - organizational factors?
  - the personal psychologies of the individuals?

Decisions

3 Review these solutions. Decide which might help John.

(a) Have someone make a rubber stamp that reads "TRIVIA. STOP WASTING MY TIME" and use it to stamp every item of trivia that lands on John's desk.

This will HELP because ....

This will NOT HELP because ....

(b) Have someone make a rubber stamp that reads "YOU DECIDE" and use it to stamp every item of trivia that lands on John's desk.

This will HELP because ....

This will NOT HELP because ....

(c) Ignore every item of trivia that lands on his desk.

This will HELP because ....

This will NOT HELP because ....

(d) Each week, delegate a member of staff to deal with the trivial items that land on John's desk. When every member of staff has performed this duty once, they will have learned not to waste John's time in this way.

This will HELP because ....

This will NOT HELP because ....

(e) Punish members of staff that waste time in sending items of trivia to John. If necessary, fine them.

This will HELP because ....

This will NOT HELP because ....

(f) Direct Departmental Heads that they are responsible for resolving all issues that John considers trivial.

This will HELP because ....

This will NOT HELP because ....

(g)   Only accept items of trivia for which the sender has already proposed a solution.

This will HELP because ....

This will NOT HELP because ....

(h)   Make clear that only those members of staff who do not waste John's time with trivia will be promoted or rewarded with end-of-year bonuses.

This will HELP because ....

This will NOT HELP because ....

(i)   Accept that trivia is bound to pile up in a service industry of this type, and do nothing.

This will HELP because ....

This will NOT HELP because ....

4   Propose ONE more solution that you think can help. Be prepared to justify it to others of the class.

5   Remember that even the best solution to any problem can cause new problems. What new problems might arise from the solution you proposed in 4. above?

6   Review your answer to the Case Preparation material. Do you still agree with that answer? Do you wish to change it? If YES, why?

Asia South/Research

CASE PREPARATION

Suppose that a senior post in your organization becomes vacant.

- What factors might influence you to appoint an INSIDER (existing member) of the organization?
- What factors might influence you to appoint an OUTSIDER?
- Research what happened the last time your business school appointed a new chief executive officer (who might be titled dean, director, etc.) Was an INSIDER or OUTSIDER appointed?
- What factors influenced the appointment?

Karl reread the resignation letter lying on his desk and groaned. He had some idea of how difficult it would be to make a new appointment, and was not looking forward to the effects on company morale.

The company, Asia South/Research (AS/R), was in the business of collecting and analyzing market data in the Indian sub-continent. Relevant data were then selected for the international and local non-governmental organizations who comprised the client body and communicated to them appropriately. Training courses were contracted in such areas as hygiene, pre- and post-natal care, hygiene, and small-business management.

AS/R was headquartered in San Francisco. It had been established in the late 1970s by a consortium of international charities, who still supplied the bulk of the funding. Branches were active throughout the sub-continent. Karl had taken up this post of Country Manager only ten months ago. The 38 other persons employed in this branch were all locally hired.

To date, all Country Managers had been expatriate. But before Karl had taken up this post, he had been told by the Chairman that he or (more likely) his successor was likely to be the last. One of his responsibilities was to identify a local who could be groomed for promotion to Country Manager.

At this point, the company was staffed (fragment only), as set out in figure 7.1.

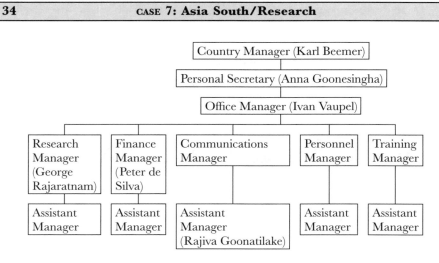

● **Figure 7.1**

Then, a few weeks ago, the Office Manager, Ivan Vaupel, was knocked down by a hit-and-run driver, and hospitalized. Ivan had been in place as the senior local staff member since AS/R was established in the late 1970s. His physician had advised that he spend six months resting at home, and given his age, he felt he had no alternative but to retire.

Checking through the records, Karl was astonished to discover that not one of the other senior staff, the five departmental managers, had been with the company for less than ten years.

This group of top managers had seen expatriate Country Managers come and go every two or three years. None matched the expatriates in academic or managerial qualifications. But Karl was beginning to realize that if they thought a Country Manager misguided, they were quite likely to ignore or reinterpret his (or headquarters) policies. They were always able to command greater loyalty than the expatriate.

Because they worked easily together, their junior staffs were also able to communicate easily. Karl realized that he could not take much of the credit for the good relationships and high morale.

He wished that he had been briefed on making local appointments in this particular country. After some thought, he decided to invite both internal and external applications. He explained the procedures to local staff in a meeting, making clear that all applications would be judged by the same criteria, and that internal applicants could not expect preferential treatment. The job was advertised in the local English-language Press and on the office bulletin board.

He announced that six weeks after the advertisements had appeared, he alone would interview all candidates and make the final selection.

Although managerial pay levels are considerably lower than in multinational and local industry, the company enjoyed high local status. Over thirty applications were received, of which thirteen should be considered seriously. As he had learned to expect, most of the external applications were male, although one good female application came in. After some thought, Karl recognized the name.

Lakshmi Pieris had been personal secretary to his predecessor, Dwight. The one day between Karl's arrival and Dwight's departure had been quite inadequate for Dwight to say much about the staff other than introducing those presently in post, but Dwight had mentioned Lakshmi. "This is a small social world and she's well-connected, you're certainly going to run into her at some party. She's very intelligent." A short time after moving into the post, Karl had met her at an Embassy reception.

A mutual acquaintance had seen them talking together, and later asked, "She told you that she was one of the old-timers, joined almost at the start?"

"Yes, then a couple of years ago she was getting stale and went to work for her brother."

"Dwight used to swear by her, as sharp as a razor and very efficient. She seemed to know everybody's job as well as they did. She knows where all the skeletons are buried. That made some of her colleagues very nervous. They weren't sorry to see her go."

Her post had been filled by Anna Goonesingha, an external appointment. Anna still lacked experience and confidence, but Karl was sure that in time she would develop into a very useful member of the team.

Now Lakshmi's brother had gone into bankruptcy, and she was applying to return to AS/R, although to the higher level post. She missed the close relationships that were such a feature of AR/S.

Other external applications included one from an ex-police inspector, who lacked experience using research material, and the marketing manager of a Japanese-owned company. There were two from foreigners. One came from an American PhD, who by chance had graduated from the same Mid West university as Karl, and whom he had met occasionally at official meetings. This woman had previously served in a senior post with the United Nations in Bangkok, and her work was respected, but she had no experience of the Indian sub-continent.

The second foreign application came from a Scottish school teacher who had thirty years' experience of working in different schools and training colleges around the region.

Karl was surprised by the excitement within the company, and the explosion of interest that followed the formal invitation for applications. Staff lunch breaks were taken up with the animated discussion of who could be expected to apply and who should be appointed. He realized that the absence of any moves in the senior levels of the company for so many years was an important factor.

In the event, three internal applications came. George Rajaratnam was Research Manager. He was a solid professional with a distant manner and a reputation for high ethical and professional standards, respected throughout the company but with no close friends. He could take unpopular decisions, and seemed impervious to other people's opinions. His family had migrated here from the West coast of India, and he was a practising Christian – unlike most of his colleagues. Whereas the other managers and their families socialized with each other outside the workplace, his appearance at a social occasion was relatively infrequent.

Peter de Silva, the Finance Manager, was a very different personality. Whereas George was conservative and cautious, Peter loved to dream up new projects, even when these had no immediate bearing on his own function. He had recently proposed that the company develop new teaching programs in small-business management, and start employing their own teachers rather than contracting out. He had a reputation for wanting complete control over every new project, and then delegating when he began to lose interest. He liked to be friendly with everybody and in social occasions usually managed to make himself the centre of a group. When frustrated or forced into situations where he felt himself losing face, he displayed a sharp temper.

Rajiva Goonatilake was at the next rank down, Assistant Communications Manager. Nobody was surprised that he decided to apply. He was thought of as the rising star, clever and hard working. He took no trouble to hide his ambition, and this irritated his superiors. In addition to a good degree from an American university, he had come to the company with several years' field experience in projects across the country. By now he had been in his present position for two years, but was sometimes guilty of making managerial decisions too quickly and without sufficient judgment.

Privately, Karl thought that in time he should be the first local to be appointed Country Manager. Before that, however, he needed to spend time working in the San Francisco headquarters.

The letters began to arrive as soon as the first applications came in. Karl returned from lunch to find a sealed envelope on his desk.

"Dear Sir: In reference to your advertised post, I have unhappy information that I feel is my moral obligation to communicate. Mr Peter de Silva is by no means the figure of integrity that he pretends to be. Project costings are regularly inflated, so craftily that even a person of your renowned diligence is unlikely to find the discrepancy. Small sums regularly disappear from petty cash . . ."

And so on. Accusations of fraud, theft, sexual indiscretion, and mismanagement were made against all the internal and some of the external candidates. All were anonymous. On three occasions, phone calls were made to his house late in the evening. He did not recognize their voices but felt sure that these callers were being briefed by members of the company. He could identify some of his correspondents. A letter accusing Lakshmi Pieris of sexual immorality had apparently been dictated by her replacement, Anna Goonesingha.

Not all the letters and calls were negative. Extravagent recommendations were also made, praising the energy and ethical integrity of this candidate or that.

As time went on, it became clear that groups were forming around the various internal candidates. In general, the research staff stayed loyal to George, and finance staff to Peter. Rajiva's candidacy had split the other three departments. The younger and junior staff favoured him, but their seniors were the most committed to either George or Peter. Apparently none of the long-term staff hoped for Lakshmi's return, but she had some support among the junior staff – particularly among a group of female secretaries who had a grievance against Anna.

No one doubts that Rajiva is by far the best and most experienced of the five Assistant Managers in the company.

At lunch times the various factions went off to eat by themselves. Relations within the company were souring, and Karl sensed that the flow of information was no longer as easy and automatic as it had been.

There were no signs that output had fallen, and only the day before one of their main clients had expressed himself delighted (as usual) with the quality of work and speed of delivery. However, it seemed obvious that this competition would have an adverse effect on staff morale and efficiency if it were prolonged for much longer. Anna had let slip to him that a serious argument had broken out between the Assistant Managers of Research and Finance over a research budget and materials allocations for research staff. Karl asked her to ask them to come to see him, but she seemed to think that it would be best if they sorted it out between themselves, and he let the matter drop.

On the day of the interviews, Karl sat down to review the applications for the last time. He was still uncertain over which candidate was the best – on paper. He hoped that the eventual decision would put an end to the feuding. There had been no complains about the appointments procedure. Nevertheless, he began to wonder whether a better system could be devised.

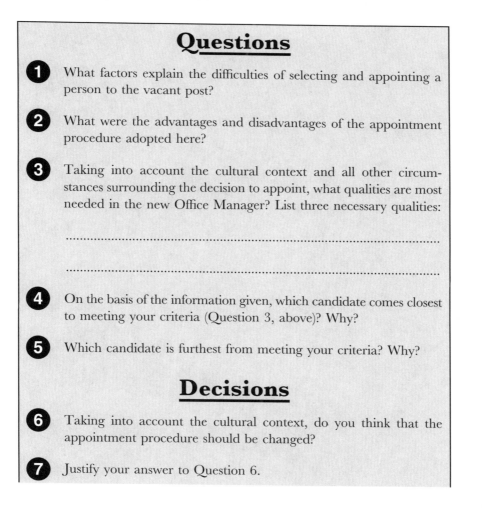

Questions

1 What factors explain the difficulties of selecting and appointing a person to the vacant post?

2 What were the advantages and disadvantages of the appointment procedure adopted here?

3 Taking into account the cultural context and all other circumstances surrounding the decision to appoint, what qualities are most needed in the new Office Manager? List three necessary qualities:

....

....

4 On the basis of the information given, which candidate comes closest to meeting your criteria (Question 3, above)? Why?

5 Which candidate is furthest from meeting your criteria? Why?

Decisions

6 Taking into account the cultural context, do you think that the appointment procedure should be changed?

7 Justify your answer to Question 6.

(a) If you think the procedure should be changed, why? What change(s) should be made? Analyse the problem(s) in the existing procedure and propose solutions, using the following headings.

- Problem(s).
- Causes of the problems.
- First solution proposed:
  Advantages and disadvantages.
- Second solution proposed:
  Advantages and disadvantages.
- Solution chosen from the two above:
  Reasons for choice.

OR

(b) If you think the procedure should NOT be changed, why not? What are the possible alternatives and why might they be less successful than the existing procedure?

honesty and ethics

Story 1   Marelika at Work

In her first job, Marelika worked as an assistant marketing manager. She belonged to a team whose other members were Haansi, Mayuri and Colbert. One day, she was alone in the office while they attended a sales conference. By mistake she recontracted a direct mailing agency whose record had proved disappointing. Her boss had told them all before that they should not recontract, and when he discovered what had happened he was furious.

"This is going to cost us money which we can't afford. Were you responsible?" he challenged Marelika.

Marelika chose between the following responses.

ALTERNATIVE RESPONSES

(a)   "Yes."
(b)   "No."
(c)   "We take all decisions jointly. Haansi, Mayuri and Colbert are also responsible."

1   Rate these responses in terms of:
HONESTY. Which is most honest? Second most honest? Least honest?
ETHICS. Which is most ethical? Second most ethical? Least ethical?

Story 2   Marelika and her Father

Marelika's father was an old man, but he loved life and someone of his age and condition could normally look forward another ten years of activity. Then without warning, he was struck by illness. Marelika called a doctor. After examining the old man, the doctor led Marelika outside the bedroom and confided in her, "It is probable that your father will die within the next two months."

When the doctor had left, the old man called her into the room.

"What did he say?" he asked.

ALTERNATIVE RESPONSES

(d)   Marelika said nothing.

(e)   "Daddy, he said that you will probably die within the next two months."

(f)   "Daddy, great news. So long as you take your medicine and are sensible about resting and what you eat and wear, you can look forward to another ten good years."

2   Rate these responses in terms of
HONESTY. Which is most honest? Second most honest? Least honest?
ETHICS. Which is most ethical? Second most ethical? Least ethical?

Story 3   Marelika and Karos in Love

The old man died, and Marelika was alone in the world. She then acquired a boyfriend, Karos. They were very happy together, and planned to marry. After several months, though, Marelika had second thoughts. She knew that he loved her, more than ever. But she no longer shared his interests and she felt increasingly oppressed by their relationship. She had fallen out of love. It was nobody's fault. Finally she decided to break off the engagement.

ALTERNATIVE BEHAVIORS

(g)   Without saying a word to Karos, Marelika disappeared. She moved to a new city and made sure that he would never find her.

(h)   "I have decided to break off our engagement. Goodbye."

(i)   "I know that you love me, more than ever. But I no longer share your interests and I feel increasingly oppressed by our relationship. I have fallen out of love. It is nobody's fault. I am breaking off our engagement. Goodbye."

(j) "Karos, I love you more and more, and I'm becoming more jealous every day. I do not want you to talk to any other women, or even to look at them." At first Karos is flattered by her pretended attention. Then she says, "Karos, I feel insecure every time you leave home. Some other woman may decide to take you, and that you may not be strong enough to resist. Forgive me, but I cannot help myself." They have a number of rows, always caused by Marelika's pretended jealousy. Finally Karos says, "I know that you love me but we cannot continue like this. I feel oppressed. We should break off our engagement. I am sorry. I hope that we can continue to be friends. Goodbye."

Marelika says, "I understand, and you are right, we cannot continue. It is my fault. And yes, I shall always think of you as my dear friend."

3 Rate these responses in terms of:
HONESTY. Which is most honest? Second most honest? Third most honest? Least honest?
ETHICS. Which is most ethical? Second most ethical? Third most ethical? Least ethical?

4 Which of these responses (g, h, i, j) would Marelika be most SENSIBLE to pursue? Why?

Story 4 Marelika and Karos in Business

Marelika found a job abroad and forgot Karos. Three years later she was sent back to her country to negotiate an important contract with a client. If she succeeded in obtaining the concessions her company needed, she would be promoted to the board. But if she failed, she would lose her job. She know that the other side had the stronger hand, but she was sure that she could use her charm and intelligence successfully. Excited by the challenge, she strode into the client's boardroom to meet her negotiation partner. She knew that he was a considered a brilliant high flier, but had not been given his name. Then he came in and she looked at him – it was Karos!

5 How would you expect Karos to behave, supposing that Marelika had previously chosen:

   response g?
   response h?
   response i?
   response j?

6 Given your answers to 5, do you wish to change your answer to 4? IF YES, change them.

7 IF the events in Story 4: have persuaded you to change your answer to 4, do you think that your decision to change is

honest? Why?

ethical? Why?

8 (l)   Check your answers to a–k with members of your own culture group. How far do you agree? What factors explain agreements? Disagreements?

   (m)   Check the answers to a–k given by members of some other culture group. How far do they agree among themselves? What factors explain agreements? Disagreements?

   (n)   How far do the answers given by your culture group, and by their culture group, agree? What factors explain agreements? Disagreements?

9 Define "ethical behavior". What sort of behavior is ethical? What sort of behavior is unethical?

10 Review your answer to the Case Preparation material. Do you still agree with that answer? Do you wish to change it? If YES, why?

the Swiss–Thai joint venture

CASE PREPARATION

Assume that you have been appointed manager of a joint venture formed between a local partner company and a foreign partner company. You have been posted from the foreign partner and the venture is based in the country of the foreign partner.

What problems might arise in communications between the partners, and between partners and the project?

Discuss your answer with other members of the class. Agree on a list of possible problems.

A Swiss company, Portozen, established a joint venture with two Thai partners. The Bangkok-based project aimed to research and market the development of industrial ceramics in Southeast Asia.

The Thai partners had their primary business interests in real estate and insurance. In their early meetings with Portozen they emphasized that they were only interested in ceramics for the investment possibilities. They said that they could take Portozen's technological expertise on trust. They would provide support in securing office space and advising on recruitment. One of their partners, the real estate firm, contributed an accountant to the project team. Otherwise, they seemed unwilling to involve themselves in day-to-day operations. The Swiss were given the impression that they were being freed to manage the project as though it were a subsidiary – on condition that the financial targets were met.

It was negotiated that the project should be located in Bangkok. All project communication between the parents was to be routed through the project manager.

Eva was appointed to this post. She had trained as an industrial chemist and after eight years work experience as a technician and manager had taken an international MBA in a French management school. This was her first major appointment abroad, and she was anxious to make a success of it. A ceramic engineer, Rolf, was appointed to consult with the project in its first three months.

The other twelve members of the team were Thai, recruited through links with the Thai Development and Research Institute.

Eva had travelled in Asia during student vacations, but this was her first working assignment outside Europe. When she had arrived, her new subordinates had already found her an excellent service apartment within easy reach of the project offices on Soi Ton Son Road. They entertained her in the city's best restaurants and showed her around the tourist sights. At 33 years old, Eva was the oldest member of the project team. She was eager to establish good working relations with the project staff. In her first full meeting with project staff, Eva assured them: "If you have any complaints, any suggestions, and queries, please come and talk to me. My office door is always open." They looked at each other and said nothing.

At first, Eva's invitation to confide met with no response. The staff apparently preferred to keep her at a cool distance, as a superior who should be treated with deference. Then one day, she returned from lunch with a business acquaintance to find them sitting in a group around one of their desks discussing a bulletin from her head office. One of the marketing staff, Charnvit was translating it into Thai for the benefit of a secretary whose competence in reading English was weak. "Tha raaw mee phanhaa . . ."

"If we have problems," said Eva.

They looked at her with surprise.

"Dichan rian phuut phasaa Thai", she said. "I'm learning to speak Thai."

After that, the atmosphere changed. Eva began to win their confidence. They shared their snacks, and at lunchtimes she went out with them to the local restaurants. They began to come to her with questions and queries. Soon she was spending a great part of the working day explaining headquarters procedures. Often, these were relatively minor points which were quickly forgotten. Again and again she had to insist on project members coming properly prepared to meetings, arriving on time and not overrunning.

It became apparent that production in the available plant would lead to cost overruns and that market demand needed to be recalculated. Delay was inevitable. Then Santi, the accountant, seemed to become very interested in the technical processes of manufacturing industrial ceramics. A few days before returning to Geneva, Rolf complained about the questions he was being asked. "Every day he's after something new. Today it was temperatures in the annealing process. What's he on about? He's way outside his area of responsibility."

"Does he understand what you tell him?"

"Not always. He makes notes."

Eva asked, "What happens after next week? When you have gone."

Rolf smiled. "You have to come up with the answers. And I warn you, he won't take no for an answer."

"I'll e-mail you."

"Yes. Or tell him to contact me directly."

After Rolf had flown back, Eva began to realize that Santi was asking questions that he often did not understand himself. He was asking on behalf of a third person, and she guessed that Santi was being fed the questions by his boss in the real estate company. She was annoyed. If the partners were losing confidence in Portozen technology, they should make their new position clear. She decided that the best way to resolve the issue was to supply a full set of the relevant literature.

"They have the technical specifications for the project," her line manager replied.

"I know that. But they want more. They're looking to understand the technology."

A day later Eva received a call from her managing director in Portozen head-quarters. "What's this about?" he demanded, and when Eva had explained he sounded worried.

"Are they asking for proprietory material? We have to worry about intellectual property rights . . ."

She tried to allay his fears. "No, I don't think it's that and nor does Rolf. It's rather an issue of face."

"What?"

"They're realizing now that they've made a heavy investment in a business that they don't understand."

"That issue arose when we negotiated. They were happy to accept the technology on trust. We can advise on a qualified consultant."

But Eva understood that the Thai partners were unlikely to trust a consultant recommended by Portozen.

"And they do trust an accountant? Who has no other technical qualifications?"

"They know their accountant."

"They know me, they signed the contract with me. Only last week I spoke to them and asked if they had any problems. They said they were happy."

The next day he called again. "I want to know about your Mr Santi. Is he asking for this information in project meetings?"

"Always on a one-to-one basis."

"Why not in meetings? I've been going over your meeting report. They seem to cover procedural matters in great detail and not much else."

Eva tried to explain differences between Thai and Swiss priorities in making and implementing plans. "Long-term planning is difficult here."

"How long do your meetings last? On average? . . . Why so long? . . . Well, why don't they arrive on time?"

Eva had been managing the joint venture for a year. As the weeks ran on, Mr Santi dropped the pretence of seeking technical detail for his own interest, and introduced an engineer working for the parent company. The Thais were worried by cost-overruns, and needed continual assurances that these were inavoidable and that the project was on course. Meanwhile, headquarters staff too were query-ing project progress and procedures. Eva's evenings were spent in explaining and defending Thai values to uncomprehending Swiss engineers who had no experi-ence of non-European cultures.

Eva was exhausted. She felt herself torn between two sides, neither of which understood the other or entirely trusted her. She wondered how long she could stand up to the pressure.

Questions

 1 Which of these factors are causing problems for the joint venture?

Choose the three most important factors, and explain why each is important.

(a) The partners do not understand each other's business interests. YES / NO.

(b) Eva is a bad manager, and needs management training. YES / NO.

(c) Eva made a mistake in learning Thai, and then telling her staff. YES / NO.

(d) Mr Santi lacks the technical qualifications needed by someone with his functional responsibilities. YES / NO.

(e) The project lacks agreed systems and priorities for communicating between partners. YES / NO.

(f) The Thai partners do not understand Swiss culture. YES / NO.

(g) The Swiss partner does not understand Thai culture. YES / NO.

(h) The Thai staff do not like planning. YES / NO.

(i) The Swiss and Thai partners have different goals for the project. YES / NO.

(j) (Your suggestion ....)

2 Discuss your choices with other students. Together, prepare a presentation analysing the problems facing the joint venture.

Decisions

3 Which of the problems might have been prevented at the time when the joint venture was negotiated?

4 How might the problems have been resolved, or at least lessened, after the first year of Eva's appointment?

Consulair

CASE PREPARATION

You manage a small plastics company (300 employees) based outside Chicago. The organizational culture is positive and strong. You are considering forming a joint venture with a petroleum company based in Europe. The joint venture will develop and market a new industrial paint to the eastern European economies, you hope over a five year period. You have been examining proposals made by two German and one French companies. Which do you choose? Why?

Company:	OskarBroe	PGMPetrol	FargenGas
Country:	Germany	Germany	France
Employees:	18000	300	300
Management style:	Participatory	Hierarchical	Patriarchal
Previous IJV history:	Wide experience in East Asia	Some experience in the USA and eastern Europe	Some experience in western Europe
Proposed time-scale:	Five years	Five years	Four years

What other factors might influence your choice? Discuss your answers with members of the class, and agree on a list:

(a) ....

(b) ....

(c) ....

(d) ....

"I certainly hope that we can do business with this company," said Dr Richard Hauptmann, the chairman of Mainz/Schugel (M/S). "I have had my eye on the Latin-American market for some time. And this gives us the opening we need. But first I want you to pay them a visit. You know the sort of things to look for. How easy will it be to cooperate with them? What managerial commitments should we expect to make? How easily can they mesh with our culture?"

Liza Wing Khoi-peng nodded and made a note. She had seen the correspondence with Pedro Terry, chairman and sole owner of Consulair, Peru. She knew that her boss had already commissioned a marketing survey and report on Consulair, and that her task would be to assess the implications for management and communication systems.

Once before M/S had entered a joint venture outside Europe; but the problems of cross-cultural communication had led to serious problems. The experience had not been forgotten, and senior M/S managers reacted cautiously when Dr Hauptmann had announced his interest in Consulair. In particular, the senior production staff had been apprehensive when it became clear that they would be involved in developing new production lines with the partner. He realized that they did not share his enthusiasm for the deal, and so decided to send the best of his young business analysts to make an assessment of the situation.

Liza was the bright daughter of a poor Chinese family that had emigrated to Germany shortly after her birth. She had been brought up in the German educational system, and spoke German as her first language. Now 30 years old, Liza had worked in this Berlin-based telecommunications firm for five years.

Consulair manufactured air-conditioning units for use in large service plants – for instance, factories, hotels, and hospitals. Net profits were still very healthy; 7 percent on the previous year. But this compared with an 11 percent margin on the year before, itself 15 percent up on the year before that. Terry explained these figures by his conviction that the air-conditioning market was beginning to mature. He had decided that he needed to further diversify his interests.

He had been looking for an opportunity to move into a higher technology. A conversation with a hospital administrator had convinced him that he should aim for local assembly of computerized hospital technologies, and sales throughout Latin America. But he needed a partner. After talking with family members he decided to approach a distant relative on his wife's side, and this person had put him into touch with Dr Hauptmann. They had met in New York and again in Berlin (while Liza was away visiting a trade fair), and the joint venture had been proposed.

Dr Hauptmann was much impressed by the younger man's energy and knowledge of local markets – although also taken aback by his Latin exuberance and lack of reserve. Terry returned home with an understanding that the chances of reaching agreement on a joint venture were good.

The market survey contracted by M/S concluded that, if anything, Terry had underestimated the opportunities for the proposed technologies.

The day after being briefed, Liza boarded the flight to Peru. This was the first time that she had visited Latin America, and she was excited to be making the trip.

She was met at the airport by Franco, Terry's personal aide. On the drive into Lima, he said that Terry was waiting to greet her. On their arrival at the company, he was put out to discover that his boss was not in the office. He filled in the time by giving her a brief history of the company.

Consulair had been established six years before. At first, the only employees had been Terry and two friends. They were all untrained in business and lacked experience, but made up for this with energy and imagination. They very quickly became successful, and soon signed a licensing agreement with a Belgian firm that was looking for an adventurous local partner. The two friends had moved on to other activities, and Terry was left in sole control. Within three years Consulair was employing 240 persons. This figure had since risen to nearly 400.

"How is the firm structured?" Liza asked. Franco produced an organizational chart (figure 10.1).

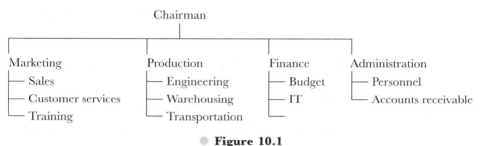

● **Figure 10.1**

He was summoned out of the room for a few minutes, which gave Liza time to examine the chart. On his return she asked, "Why is Training under Marketing rather than in Personnel?"

"Oh, Personnel do their own training. They also arrange training for the Finance and Production departments."

"And so Training only services Marketing?"

"That keeps them busy enough. Sales, Customer services, Purchasing and Training alone account for over 200 people."

Liza examined the chart again and asked, "Where's Purchasing?"

"Yes, that's a new department, and we haven't got round to revising the chart yet. Morales, the Production Manager, used to do all the purchasing himself, then some serious mistakes were made. Eventually the Chairman got fed up with the problems and a couple of months ago he decided to set up a new department."

"But why is it under Marketing? Why not Production?"

"You'll have to ask the chairman about that. Anyway, Morales is going to leave so it doesn't matter."

"Right, now let me get this straight. The Training Department services Marketing and these other departments."

"They also offer some programs to Production."

"Doesn't that bring Personnel and Training into conflict?"

"It used to be worse. Then the old Personnel Manager quit, and her replacement, Rosaria, makes a point of keeping good relations across the company. In fact she and Velasco – he's the Training Manager – are working together on the Production programs."

He hesitated. "It's my feeling that Personnel would like to be free of all training responsibilities."

"Why is that?"

"Because they feel overloaded. The boss wants them to develop some practical system for appraising performance."

"Well – surely you have a system?"

"When the firm was small and everyone knew everyone else, it wasn't necessary. Then there was too much to do and no one had the time. The boss gave it some thought, and so did his mother . . ."

"His mother? She is a manager here?"

"No, of course, not. But she always gives advice to the boss. They both have other interests. Of course, the supervisors do their best, but they can't agree on what's important."

"So will the chairman agree to Personnel giving up training?"

"There's no reason why not. He lets his managers sort out the details, as far as they can."

"Suppose they don't agree?"

"He can't do everything. He doesn't want to be bothered with disputes at that level. It's much better that individuals sort out their own differences without taking up his time."

"And if you asked for his help?"

"Then of course he would go out of his way to help. But he is a very important man. We do not like to bother him."

"I look forward to meeting him."

"Yes, he sends his deepest apologies for the delay. I have just heard that there has been an emergency at one of the warehouses. The fire precautions have to be a priority."

"On air-conditioning units?"

"No, no, this is imported brandy. Another of his businesses. He is always worried about a fire breaking out."

The next day a secretary came to Liza's temporary office to inform her that the chairman was in his office and would like to meet her.

"Thank you, I'll just finish looking over this file and come up in ten minutes."

The secretary looked acutely embarrassed. "No, he's here now."

Obviously, an invitation to meet the chairman was equivalent to an order. When she reached the executive floor she found him talking to one of his executive secretaries. Liza reflected that even Dr Hauptmann, who was greatly respected by his employees as a fair man and a good professional, could not expect to be treated with so great a degree of unquestioning deference.

He looked a little surprised when she was introduced, and took her through to his private office.

"I will tell you frankly, Ms Wing Khoi-peng, I assumed that Dr Hauptmann would send a man. And of course your Chinese name gives nothing away." He smiled. "Here, I am always the last person to know. No one tells me anything."

She laughed, finding him easy to talk to.

As she had expected, Terry wanted to spend time in general discussion. He showed interest in her professional experiences and qualifications. Dr Hauptmann had told her that he was a cultured man. Before flying over she had made a point of finding out about Latin-American literature, in particular Peruvian writing, and she was able to ask him some intelligent questions. He was clearly pleased that she had made the effort.

After about an hour, he cleverly edged the conversation towards the proposed joint venture. Liza was able to show that she was in Dr Hauptmann's confidence, and this seemed to increase his sense of confidence in talking to her. She explained that there was no doubting that the goals of the two companies in planning this joint venture seemed to complement each other excellently.

And the commercial success of Consulair was obvious.

"However, I am here on slightly different business, to start planning management systems in the proposed joint venture. Our managers place great emphasis on matching organizational cultures when we go into an alliance and how the two parents can communicate effectively."

He looked puzzled for a moment. "Well, I am sure that Dr Hauptmann and I can communicate very well."

"Well, for instance, if our production manager has a problem working with your team, with whom should he communicate?"

"We are an open company. Anyone who has a problem is free to discuss it with me. If a problem such as that arose, I should of course advise my staff, then if necessary take it up directly with Dr Hauptmann."

Liza was aware that the two bosses had struck up a good personal relationship.

"Please do not think that I am distrustful of my managers. They are all people of integrity whom I personally selected. They work very hard. Of course problems arise and they do make mistakes. But that is only because they are young and lack management expertise. They could benefit from further training."

She was interested in where he thought training could be most beneficial, and produced the copy that Franco had made for her of the organizational chart. He took a quick look and said, "This is out of date."

"I know. Franco explained about the new Purchasing Department . . ."

"And Sales. I've decided to separate Home Sales and Foreign Sales. But Franco doesn't know about that."

The discussion drifted into questions of management training, which Liza did not think was of immediate importance, and she left to write up her notes.

The next day, she returned to his office to ask for an introduction to the factory. The secretary said "I'm sure that there will be no difficulty. But I have to ask the Chairman to sign a note for you. If you would take a seat . . ."

Five minutes later, the secretary emerged with an envelope which she gave to Liza. She then spoke to another woman who had also been waiting.

Liza and the other woman left the secretary's office together. The other woman gave a wry smile and said, "he wants me to come back tomorrow. He's had to go out to look at a business he hopes to buy." She introduced herself as Teresa Maria Berlan, Manager of the Customer Services Department. As they sat together over a coffee, she explained why she had wanted to see Terry.

When customers wished to question their accounts, they often telephoned Accounts Receivable first. This was a mistake. Customer Services were responsible for investigating all aspects of a complaint, including queries over accounts, and so many complaints received by Accounts Receivable had to be transferred to Customer Services.

Relations between the two departments had been poor for many years. The initial cause of the conflict was uncertain; it certainly predated Teresa Maria, who had been with the company for only two years. Recently, Accounts Receivable had been asked to sort out problems which they claimed had nothing to do with them, and this was adding unnecessarily to their work load. In retaliation they had started a policy of giving misleading answers to wrong calls, or hanging up on them. A major customer had threatened to take his business elsewhere, and now Customer Services were being blamed for the discourteous service. The Manager of Accounts Receivable had promised to meet with Teresa Maria "sometime soon" to sort things out, but could never find the time. In desperation, she had decided to ask Terry to resolve the problems.

"Everyone respects him. In many ways he's an excellent manager. He can be very helpful when you have a difficulty. But he gets angry if you take up his time with day-to-day details, if he thinks you ought to be able to find the answer yourself, or if he's bored.

But I think I'm going to have to tell him what's going on. Either that or I have to quit. And I don't want to do that. I love my work and I really enjoy working for a man like him. There's always something new happening. I'm not like Julio Cesar and Alfredo – you heard about them?"

Liza had heard something of these two managers who had recently quit.

"The ones who can't cope, they choose to go. The boss doesn't want to sack anyone – if he can help it."

"Weren't they qualified?"

"They had experience, and MBA degrees – like most of us. No, just their management style was wrong. I'm not like them, I'm one of those who try to be entrepreneurial in our thinking, like the boss. But sometimes all this change is too much and I feel as though everything's out of control. That's depressing. What do you think I should do?"

Liza made some excuse about needing more time to think. The next day she was taken on a tour of the plant. She had been led to expect a degree of inefficiency and waste that would not have been acceptable in Germany. She was amazed. Allowing for restrictions on capital investment, production processes were well-planned and efficient. The supervisors and workers with whom she had a chance to talk were skilled and interested in what they were doing, and more important from her point of view, interested in learning new skills. She was confident that M/S production staff would have no problems working with them.

That evening in the hotel, she opened her laptop computer and prepared to draft her report. She hesitated. The experiences of the past few days had left her feeling extremely confused.

Questions

1 Why was Liza confused?

2 What evidence is there of bad communication within Consulair? How do you explain this?

3 What further information should Liza search for?

4 How do you explain the dispute between Customer Services and Accounts Receivable? How can it be resolved?

5 M/S is headquartered in Germany. Consulair is headquartered in Peru. Liza is Chinese by birth. How far were differences between German, Peruvian and Chinese cultures responsible for the problems?

Decision

6 You are a consultant retained by Mainz/Schugel (M/S). Dr Richard Hauptmann has read Liza's report with interest. He now asks you:

   On what conditions should we enter a joint venture with Consulair?
   On what conditions should we NOT enter a joint venture with Consulair?

Advise.

an American family company

CASE PREPARATION

In all capitalist countries, family companies make major contributions to the economy. In what respects do family companies differ around the world? As an exercise, research recruitment policies in:

    traditional Chinese family companies in Hong Kong.
    American family companies in the United States.

In each type:

  A Under what conditions might the company owner employ family members as managers in preference to outsiders?
  B What problems are perceived to arise from employing outsiders?
  C Under what conditions might the owner employ outsiders as managers in preference to family members?
  D What problems are perceived to arise from employing family members?

Answer the same four questions for YOUR country.

Discuss your answers with other members of the class.

In Chicago in 1958, Cyril K. Edwardes borrowed $400 to develop hair products for African-Americans. In the first year, the company employed only Cyril, his wife Ruth, and his brother Jacob. As the company grew and outsiders were recruited, the great majority of the staff came from the same poor Southside suburb in which Cyril and his family had grown up.

In 1963 Cyruth Industries' products were being marketed widely. Similar products had been developed a few years earlier by another black-owned firm, Jackson Products. Nevertheless, Cyruth was a huge success. In 1974 a limited public stock offering made it one of the first black-owned family business to trade on the American Stock Exchange.

Three years later, sales hit $45.7 million. Cyril acted as President and Chief Executive Officer. Ruth was appointed Chief Financial Officer and Jacob Sales Director. The production and personnel functions were managed by long-standing family friends.

But by the late 1980s, growth was slowing and sales were falling. The company was still outsold by Jackson Products and more recent competitors such as Clairol, Revlon and the French firm Maria-Syncho (who had earlier made a bid) were taking market share. This competition had forced Cyruth to expand too rapidly outside its home territories of the mid-west and as a result, distribution problems were multiplying.

In the south and south-west retailers increasingly complained that orders were misprocessed and deliveries were not made. There were matching difficulties of hiring and training a competent sales force. Too often, those sales people who did show themselves able to make an impression were immediately hired away by a competitor. As a result, morale at headquarters was falling.

By 1993 the company had suffered four losses in the previous six fiscal years. Jacob resigned on grounds of ill-health. For several years, Cyrus had been in poor health. He was anxious to retire from day-to-day operations, and the crisis prompted him to take that step.

The entire staff were invited to a farewell banquet. Cyrus announced what had been an open secret. He was making his second son, Jason, President and Chief Operating Officer. The eldest boy, Edwin, practised as a physician, and after a few months working with his father a decade before had vowed that he would never repeat the experience and if possible never leave New York.

Jason began a process of reorganization and acquired a small retail chain that proved highly profitable a few years later. This helped resolve immediate sales and distribution problems and the corner was turned. In 1996 the previous losses had been recovered. The company was back in profit and Jason was lauded as the hero.

At this point Edwin returned from New York. He and his father spent several hours in close conversation, at the end of which they announced to family members that their personal problems were resolved. From henceforth, Edwin would take on a consulting role in the company, reporting directly to his father. Jason bit his lip. "What does that mean?" he asked. "Office space," his father explained. "When he has time from his practice he will visit. You give him full access to all financial data. He will report to me. And to you."

Edwin's homecoming was supposed to be a time of family celebration and Jason did not push the issue further. He decided to wait and see whether Edwin's professed interest in the business had any depth. There was every possibility that Edwin and their father would quickly renew their old emnity. But he was surprised. This time, father and eldest son seemed happy with each other and were soon arranging fishing weekends.

In September 1996 Cyrus called Jason to a meeting. "I've looked at the figures and I've taken advice. We'll close the Stokey plant and start production in Mexico."

"Whose advice?"

"Edwin has the data."

"We need an independent consultant," Ruth suggested.

"No. Edwin is clever. And I want him in the company as Director of Operations. He feels the time is right for him to retire from medicine."

Jason resigned the following day. His departure sparked a bitter row between Cyrus and Ruth.

"Your job is to implement strategy", Cyrus said. "This is a strategy decision, it does not concern you."

"Nor you now", Ruth retorted.

Their marriage had been under strain since the late 1980s when the company had first registered. A few months later they divorced. Cyrus left the company, settling half of his stock on Ruth, who took over as chairperson. Because she already was voting trustee for the shares owned by their four grandchildren, this would give her voting power over her husband. An alternative was to sell the company and settle, but Cyrus was determined to keep the company in family hands.

Family friction increased when the second daughter, Vanessa, graduated from her liberal arts college and announced that she wanted to join the company.

"I'll start you as an assistant product manager," Ruth said. "When I think you've learned what you need to know I'll move you up, quickly."

"Daddy said I could start as a full manager."

"Daddy is no longer running the company," her mother said. "Edwin agrees with daddy."

But Ruth was adamant and Vanessa now decided against joining the company. She would prefer to see something of the world. She secured a post with Maria-Syncho in Paris. Ruth fired Edwin, and increasingly turned for advice to a non-family member hired as Chief Financial Officer.

Everyone in the local community had a relative or friend who worked for the company if they did not work for it themselves. Up to this point they had watched the comings and goings in the boardroom with equanimity. All the persons involved had been acquaintances. But Michael G. Paron was an unknown quantity. He was white, a graduate of Harvard and Arthur Andersen. His management style seemed too cold and impersonal. He sparked even greater resentment in June 1998 when he insisted on recruiting a former Andersen colleague as Director of Operations. Rumours circulated that management was about to recruit further from the same source.

"These executives only see Cyruth as another company that needs turning around," an employee complained to a community newspaper.

"They don't have the respect for it being an African-American company. They don't have feeling for the history. That's what the employees think. That's what our families and friends think."

"I've heard rumors of a strike planned," the reporter pushed.

"They aren't rumors, they're fact."

As it turned out the strike collapsed within a week. But a new mood of bitterness had been sown, from which the company never recovered. In March 1999, Ruth sold out to Linard Corp., a Los Angeles company, for about $85 million in stock. This decision was taken in the face of opposition from Cyrus, who had always vowed to keep the company within the black community.

Questions

1 How were these factors responsible for the company's rise?
(a) Family relationships.
(b) Relationships with the environment.

2 How were these factors responsible for the company's problems?
(a) Family relationships.
(b) Relationships with the environment.

3 In what respects does Cyruth Industries appear to be a typical American family company? In what respects does it not? Explain your answer.

4 What distinguishes Cyruth Industries from a traditional Chinese family company?

Decision

5 In the meeting of September 1996, Ruth suggested hiring a consultant. Suppose that you had been hired as that consultant, what advice would you have given?

Voxykoll

CASE PREPARATION

One manager, speaking at an international business conference, described his problems in decision-making thus:

Managerial decision-making is never simple. There is never adequate information. In some cases, information is insufficient; at other times I am swamped by too much information and I cannot distinguish what is important from what is trivial.

Do you agree? In your business school find examples of decisions that failed to achieve their goal because the school decision-makers:

- were unable to find sufficient information.
- were unable to distinguish important from unimportant information.

Answer the following questions:

A In what respects does the use of information technology help good decision-making?
B In what respects does the use of information technology make decision-making more difficult?

Discuss your answers with members of the class.

Voxykoll is a communications technology company, established in Dallas, Texas, in 1987. Voxykoll manufactures components used in cellular technology and sources Ericsson, Motorola and others. It has grown from its domestic base to operations in twenty one countries.

These international operations were originally structured on a transnational model. Subsidiaries were encouraged to form their own cultures independent of headquarters, and to create their own capacities for research and development. Products were differentiated and adapted on a local basis to meet local licensing requirements. At the same time, cross-unit devices integrate the whole and provided a strong international management perspective.

Over time, the more radical aspects of the structure have been modified. Global structures linking subsidiaries have given way to increasingly autonomous divisions. The regional bases of these divisions are reinforced by different product markets. Regional managers have been widely empowered.

Bill Saladol is Regional Manager for Europe. He is finding it necessary to implement different strategies in what are in practice two sub-divisions. In the developed Western economies he has decentralized controls on most functional areas other than financial systems, which is centralized. In the East European countries where the company is represented (Russia, the Czech Republic, Hungary, Poland, Romania) Bill plays a significant hands-on role in developing new operations.

By the beginning of the 1990s, all the East European countries had freed themselves from Communist control and the domination of the old Soviet Union. They had been desperate to build market economies and to join a globalized economy. This meant attracting western technology – not only the hardware but also the managerial and technical skills needed to "grow" their own private sectors. Hence they had been very favourably disposed towards technological companies like Voxykoll – provided that the local economy benefited, both from immediate financial gains and from the transfer of technology.

Bill regards these new developments as the most rewarding part of his job. But when problems arise in staffing crucial managerial functions, he finds himself making far greater commitments of time and energy than he might wish. This was certainly true in the case of an appointment in the case of Voxykill (Romania).

Romania has experienced great difficulty in moving from a centrally-administered control economy to capitalism, and by the end of the decade the subsidiary lagged some years behind its equivalents in the other East European countries. Voxykoll had been chiefly interested in developing a capacity to produce low-level circuits at low labor cost.

The original plan had been to form a joint venture and so move some of the financial and managerial commitments into local hands. But the search for a Romanian partner matching the company's specifications had been unsuccessful, and Dallas had eventually agreed with Bill's suggestion that they establish a subsidiary in which the state-owned TeleCommunications Agency (TCA) held a minority share.

Given the lack of local expertise and direct commitment, the operation had always carried a high element of risk, and it was now apparent that the initial investment had been inadequate.

The subsidiary is based in a suburb of the capital, Bucharest. The Country Manager, Jean Michel Tavernier, was posted out of the Paris subsidiary. Through no fault of his, progress has been slow.

Many of the problems spring from the chronic uncertainty affecting all departments of central government in their attempts to break with the mentality of centralized planning and to introduce systems appropriate to a market economy. The process has been difficult. Communication between government departments is frequently slow and inaccurate, and there is still a tendency for each to try acting in isolation regardless of what policies are being implemented in other departments.

The older civil servants have not been able to change their habits of thinking learned under the Communist regime, and they have no experience of handling firms in the private sector – in particular, foreign-owned firms. There is a general lack of experience in formulating and interpreting policy and legislation that relates to the private sector. Regulations are imposed and then withdrawn with great rapidity.

For instance, regulations were published last month banning expatriate spouses from taking employment within the country. Last week, employment was permitted within a few unreserved occupations. And only this morning Bill's secretary received an official fax adjusting the list.

In the circumstances, it is not surprising that government officials are nervous about giving permission for any slightly non-standard operations. They might later be forced to withdraw this permission. All this means that very considerable time and effort has to be spent in getting a new business up and running.

The local branch is now trying to recruit a Production Manager on a long-term basis. Marcus, the present Production Manager, was hospitalized with a heart attack ten days ago and there seems little hope of his returning to work.

This has come at a very bad moment. Voxykoll is tendering for a large government contract to supply the national police and armed services. The government hopes to decide on a winner by the end of the month (but a delay is quite possible). A senior TCA official telephoned this morning to commiserate, but also to underline that the government committee responsible for making the decision is looking for a company that can guarantee production. With a top-class Production Manager in place, Voxykoll stands an excellent chance of winning the contract, which should secure the subsidiary's future for the next three years – if production quotas are met. Without a top-class Manager, the company has only an even chance of winning.

In line with company policy as regards start-up ventures, the staffing request has been forwarded to Bill, as Regional Manager, for his go-ahead. This is not the first time that the subsidiary had made such a request. Six weeks ago, Anton Ionescu, the Assistant Marketing Manager, quit at short notice, soon after completing training in the German office.

In his resignation interview Anton expressed his dissatisfaction with pay differentials between himself and his expatriate Manager.

"Foreigners are paid too much. And we don't get your allowances for nice houses and nice cars," he said.

"He's a trouble maker, we're lucky to be shot of him," his Manager commented later. "There are several other hotheads about, who would like a strike."

Very soon after, it became clear that Anton had been poached by a competitor. The competitor recruited him at a higher rank – but in general, maintained similar differentials between expatriates and locals.

In that case Bill had been able to make a good local appointment. The two Assistant Managers in the Production Department are both very promising, but as yet lack the experience and skills to move into Marcus' shoes. There is no Voxykoll

Production Manager elsewhere in the region who could be moved in at such short notice, or is willing to go.

One of the obvious alternatives is to select a top-class expatriate from outside the company on a long-term contract, and half an hour ago Bill finished interviewing Ian Paron, a Briton. Ian has worked for Voxykoll before, specializing in start-up developments. He has the reputation of being a managerial star who will sooner or later graduate to a top executive post in either Europe or the United States. He knows his worth, and has the reputation of a short temper when other people's standards fall below his own.

Financial criteria are not paramount, and Bill has authority to spend what is needed (within reason) in order to get the subsidiary up to strength. But obviously, he prefers to avoid unnecessary expenditure, partly because he needs to build up his financial reserves in order to cover unforeseen ancillaries. He knows, from painful experience, that in a developing country start-up ancillaries can balloon without warning.

Headquarters is keen to secure the government contract and would prefer a strong expatriate appointment in order to facilitate control and communications. In practice, Bill works closely with Jean Michel and does not think that communication is an issue. But there is no doubting that Ian can lay the foundations of a successful production department.

Appointing Ian would be expensive. Keeping him in post will cost up to ten times the cost of a local man. He is demanding emoluments on the same level as that paid to Jean Michel. He would be accompanied by his wife and two young children, who will need local schooling. An international school 40 minutes drive from the plant seems the best possibility.

"How does your wife feel about the prospect?" Bill has asked him.

'She ought to be happy enough. Certainly she will be if she can work."

"What does she do?"

"She's a qualified accountant."

Signals from the government are mixed. The TCA is placing a premium on reaching on-stream production in the near future, and supports a top-class expatriate appointment if this can achieve the target. The Ministry of the Economy and Labor would prefer a local appointment (and has offered to assist in finding a suitable candidate), even if it leads to immediate delays in the production process. Jean Michel thinks that in time the company can adjust to either a local or expatriate appointment.

A local appointment (particularly one made from inside the company) would prove popular with local employees – many of whom agree with Anton. The Ministry has indicated that an investment in local talent would build official goodwill for the company in the future. Bill, though, is sufficiently sensitive to the political realities to realize that this cannot be guaranteed.

His immediate response to the news of Marcus' resignation was to ask Jean Michel to survey the external labor market. This was more in optimism than hope, and he is not surprised to learn that as yet no possibles have been identified.

If it were decided to hire and train a new graduate – as the Ministry seems to want – time spent in on-the-job training might be considerable. This would inevitably involve Jean Michel in some close supervision and draw him away from his other responsibilities. When trained, the new manager would demand a top local salary, and the company would have to expect their competitors to bid for the services of any person who succeeded in this difficult post.

As a stop-gap measure, the post might be offered to an expatriate on a short-term contract. Bill has spoken over the phone to an engineering manager whom he met on a previous job, Paulo Bentini. Paulo has worked in the country before (as a student), and is prepared to fly out on 24 hours' notice, but can commit himself for only three months. He will be accompanied by his wife, an artist. Bill respects his skills and his readiness to adapt to changing circumstances. Like Ian, he is a good trainer, but more tolerant of trainees who lack his own enthusiasm.

Local employees have put up with considerable disruption since the company's formation, and a period of calm would be welcomed. And TCA officials are unlikely to be happy with Paulo's relative lack of experience. He is prepared to negotiate his fee and expenses. At present he has set a figure many times higher than the local rate, although still less than the equivalent demanded by Ian.

Ian wants a quick decision, and Bill is fairly certain that offers have been made to him by at least two of their European competitors. Bill would like to take time negotiating the form of emoluments, perhaps paying a part in the form of allowances – some of which might be payable only on completion of the two-year contract. But if a decision is delayed, even by 24 hours, the opportunity to employ Ian may be lost. Bill must make a decision now.

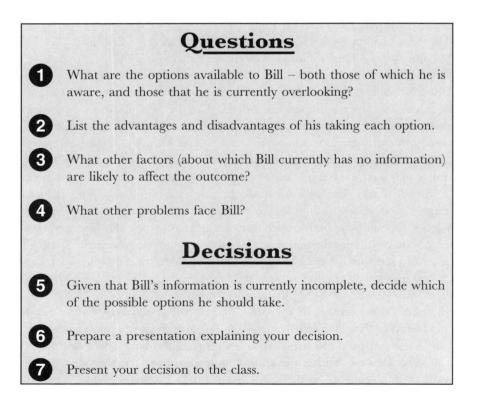

Questions

1   What are the options available to Bill – both those of which he is aware, and those that he is currently overlooking?

2   List the advantages and disadvantages of his taking each option.

3   What other factors (about which Bill currently has no information) are likely to affect the outcome?

4   What other problems face Bill?

Decisions

5   Given that Bill's information is currently incomplete, decide which of the possible options he should take.

6   Prepare a presentation explaining your decision.

7   Present your decision to the class.

the Korean hotel*

CASE PREPARATION

Imagine that your family own and manage a small hotel. Fifty years ago the great majority of your guests were tourists. Now, the overwhelming majority are business people.

Answer the following question:

What possible factors in the business environment might have caused this change? List three.

A ....

B ....

C ....

Discuss your answers with other members of the class.

In the years immediately after the Korean War the people of South Korea were occupied solely in rebuilding the basics of their shattered economy. No one had surplus money to spend, and few Koreans were sufficiently affluent to vacation away from home.

The hard work paid off. The economic boom started in the 1960s and only begun to slow down in the late 1990s. The national economy was geared to achieving developed-nation status by competing effectively in the international automobile industry.

---

* This case is based on Oh, Seong Yeob (1998); Model Hotel Management in Global Perspective: The Olympia Hotel in Ulsan, Korea. IFCOS unpublished independent study project, School of Oriental and African Studies, The University of London.

The strategy was export-driven. Competitive advantages were gained from the relatively low cost of skilled labour (that is, relative to similar industries elsewhere); nevertheless, in Korean terms income levels increased rapidly, and Korean life-styles changed. Some aspects of Western culture were borrowed and adapted to Korean needs. Koreans began to travel within the country, both on business and on vacations.

The southwestern town of Chunsan is an expanding industrial city which now has a reputation for producing quality automobile parts. In the 1960s, for-eigners visited to enjoy the peaceful and beautiful beaches, and a few Westernized Koreans also began to visit. But as the pace of industrialization increased and more factories were built, pollution took its toll and the vacation business declined steeply.

The owner of the largest hotel, the Regent, decided to sell out. He announced at a press conference that "Chunsan has become a wasteland so far as our indus-try is concerned." But not all his competitors agreed. True, they were attracting ever fewer seasonal tourists and sightseers, yet the shortfall was being made up by increasing numbers of commercial visitors, not all of them Korean. Because industry had expanded so quickly, many component technologies were unable to keep pace. Many technologies were imported, and foreign businesspeople were increasingly common in the streets where once they had been objects of curiosity. They expected to be able to meet in lobby bars and restaurants that served inter-national cuisine.

In addition, townspeople had more money to spend on hotel entertainment. Companies were willing to spend large sums on retirement parties, and families on their children's weddings.

The New World Hotel had been built by a family entrepreneur, Mr Kim Se-jon. In the early days, facilities had been limited; darkly painted bedrooms, a lobby area and a small dining room. Now that the business was beginning to make steady profits, Mr Kim began to think about extending and improving the facilities in order to serve the new clientele.

Over time, the guest profile was changing. One striking sign of this was the number of women visiting alone. Throughout the world, increasing numbers were taking up business careers, and travelling as a part of their careers. In the United States women made up only about 1 percent of all business travellers until the 1970s, but by the mid 1990s, the figure was close to 45 percent. A similar tendency was now being seen in Korea. By 1999, 37 percent of all business visitors to the New World Hotel were female.

Also, business visitors were younger, with professional qualifications. Unlike Mr Kim's generation, many had travelled outside the country, and had learned new habits. That were more conscious of the values of a healthy lifestyle.

One day, when chatting to an old friend, Mr Kim stopped to greet a regular business visitor. He commented on how fit the young man appeared.

"Yes, I've just come back from a trip to Australia."

"A vacation. I wish I had the time."

"Not quite, work. The hotel had a health club and my schedule turned out light. So I could spend a lot of time there."

"What's a health club?" he asked. He had read about them in magazine stories about the West, but had never been clear.

His guest explained, then added, "And I wasn't the only Korean there."

This time Mr Kim was really surprised. "You weren't?"

"But of course, only our young people go."

The friend interrupted. "No, no, real Koreans relax in the bath house. You'll never persuade us old-timers to change that."

"With respect," said the young man, "not only the older generation. I also like to spend time in the bath with my friends. When I come from the health club."

"Yes, that's one thing they'll never change about us Koreans," said Mr Kim, thoughtfully. "We do love the bath house."

When a journalist interviewed Mr Kim and asked about his strategy, he replied, "I don't want to talk about my strategy in detail. I'm sure that my competitors read your newspaper." "You can be sure that they'll read this interview."

Mr Kim laughed. "But I'll tell you my general attitude. In our modern world, any hotel manager has to think about what new services his customers might want. What to add, what old services that he should change or cut. He looks for signs of changing taste. Not just changing taste of one or two guests, but cultural change. New values that affect the needs of a large part of society. That part which he hopes will buy his services."

"One doesn't expect a hotelier to think so much about culture."

"Why not? Culture is always a major influence on the travel and hospitality businesses. It determines where we travel to and how, where we stay, what we eat."

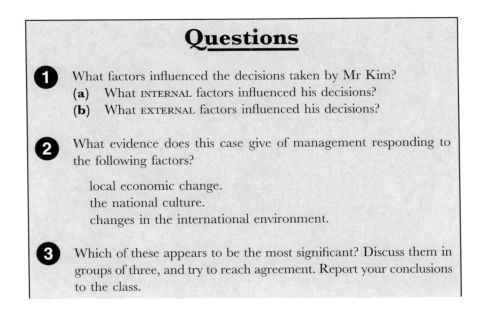

Questions

1 What factors influenced the decisions taken by Mr Kim?
 (a) What INTERNAL factors influenced his decisions?
 (b) What EXTERNAL factors influenced his decisions?

2 What evidence does this case give of management responding to the following factors?

 local economic change.
 the national culture.
 changes in the international environment.

3 Which of these appears to be the most significant? Discuss them in groups of three, and try to reach agreement. Report your conclusions to the class.

Decision

4 You are a consultant, advising the New World Hotel. The following changes have been proposed. Explain why each might, or might not, be justified. Prioritize the six most important changes:

- **(a)** Better lit mirrors in bedrooms.
- **(b)** Membership cards to all facilities.
- **(c)** A public bath.
- **(d)** A tourist desk.
- **(e)** A library and quiet reading room.
- **(f)** Rooms redorated in pastel colours.
- **(g)** A business center.
- **(h)** A bookshop.
- **(i)** Exercise rooms.
- **(j)** Tours of local attractions.
- **(k)** High quality hair driers in all bedrooms.
- **(l)** A car rental desk.
- **(m)** (any other ....)

the Australian expatriate

Paddy Ridley, an Australian management consultant, was visiting with an old client in Los Angeles. As he stood up to show his guest out, Paul Escala flipped a business card across the teak desk. "Here's an old friend who could use some help. He thinks he should talk to someone about joint venture management. I told him he can learn from you."

Paddy frowned in puzzlement. His expertise lay in analyzing organizational cultures and proposing solutions when the culture was dysfunctional. He advised companies on the dangers of a culture not directed to achieving management goals. The problems were most severe when the workforce were united in defiance of management decisions that they considered arbitrary and contrary to their interests.

"But I'm not the guy to consult on joint ventures. Paul, you know my line. But I can recommend your friend some names." And he mentioned a number of colleagues who worked in the field of joint venture management and billed in the same fee bracket. "I told him he can learn from you," Paul repeated emphatically, and refused to be drawn further. "Quin is expecting your call."

Two days later Paddy met with Quin Marrow, a fellow Australian and CEO of a medium-sized mining company.

"We're new to joint venturing and we need all the help we can get," said Marrow. "We're into a venture now, and frankly, we're having problems."

"Quin's company mined rare minerals. He had signed a deal with a Peruvian company to mount a six-month exploration and was comitted to supplying the project manager. The man posted, a long-term employee, had been a disaster. And that costs me money."

"What selection procedures do you use?"

"The best – or so we thought." He named a well-reputed local firm of consultants. "Enderek trained my human resource people in selection interview techniques. They sold us their psychometric test. The cross-cultural aptitude test. And they were expensive."

"They give value for money," corrected Paddy. "That's the best selection procedure you can buy."

"Why did you post to your 'disaster'?"

"Ed? We asked for volunteers. We used the internal electronic mail system and hard-copy notices. Everyone was circulated, but he was the only one to step forward."

"How many were eligible?"

"We've got twenty or thirty guys who we consider qualified for a job like this. They all have project experience and they're engineers. But the other's weren't interested, only Ed."

"Why not?"

Quin shrugged. "Who knows? Each individual has a private life that I know nothing about. And don't want to know."

"And none of them showed any interest? How much were you offering?"

Quin detailed the package. So far as he could judge from his limited experience of joint venture deals, Paddy thought it generous.

"They talked it out among themselves and decided not to apply. They say the money isn't good enough. But Ed's never been one of the group."

"And you had to appoint an insider? You couldn't appoint from the external market?"

"No, it had to be internal. Failing to make an internal appointment would have lost us face. And placed us in breach of contract. We had to go ahead with it. But we won't be caught like that again. That's why we came to you."

"How was Ed qualified?"

"He took the tests. His score for cross-cultural aptitude was terrible. Enderek said it was the lowest they had ever recorded. They couldn't believe it, they asked to retest. But I was not surprised."

"Why not?"

"Even here, Ed is not a good communicator. But he has strengths. He's a brilliant engineer. He has management experience. And he's loyal. We have a fairly rapid turnover, higher than the industry average, but Ed is a long-timer, he stays with the company. So we took the gamble."

"How long did he last?"

"Four weeks. By the end the Peruvians were phoning every day. The final straw was a technology problem. The Peruvians wanted to see the plans of one of our drilling bits and Ed said no. A flat no, and all the four-letter words. He should have checked with me first. I had no objections, it wasn't our newest technology and I had already promised their CEO. My R&D people agreed with me. And Ed knew that. But by then he'd decided that he didn't like our partners and wasn't about to do them any favors."

"And?"

"They demanded his recall. I had no option. Finally I told to my senior engineer to take the job, at double the money I was paying Ed. The Peruvians have met him and asked for him, he's a first-class engineer. But what they don't know is he doesn't know anything about joint-venture management. They're going to be disappointed. Then we'll be in a worse situation than ever."

"Is that how you perceive the problem?"

"Yes, whether we like it or not we have to do more joint venture work. We need joint venturing skills. First, we have no experience of working abroad. We don't have the expatriate workforce."

"An international company does not need to depend on a vast number of expatriate managers. You can build a multinational culture and have very few expatriates," said Paddy. But Quin waved him aside.

"That means we need a new selection procedure. However good the Enderek process, it isn't right for us. Second, we need advice on designing a remuneration package for expatriates. A package that brings my staff on line but doesn't bankrupt me. Third, we need training in joint venture management. Fourth . . ."

Quin broke off and smiled ruefully. "You should have stopped me. I know that the one thing consultants hate is being told what advice to give. Paul said that you were the guy to help. How do you see the problem? How can my staff learn about joint ventures?"

Paddy was about to protest that he did not normally consult on joint venture issues, when he suddenly understood why Paul had recommended him.

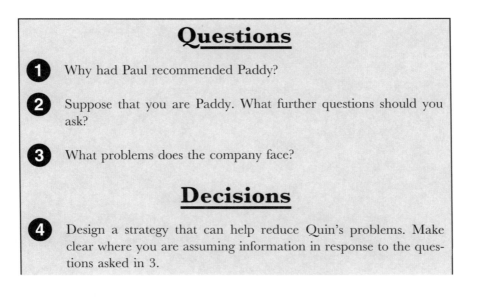

Questions

1 Why had Paul recommended Paddy?

2 Suppose that you are Paddy. What further questions should you ask?

3 What problems does the company face?

Decisions

4 Design a strategy that can help reduce Quin's problems. Make clear where you are assuming information in response to the questions asked in 3.

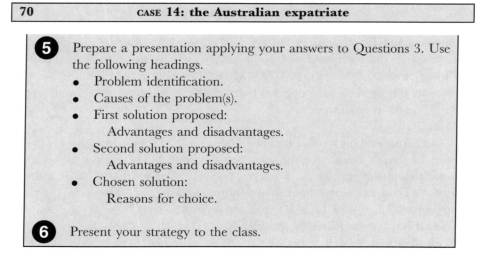

5 Prepare a presentation applying your answers to Questions 3. Use the following headings.
- Problem identification.
- Causes of the problem(s).
- First solution proposed:
    Advantages and disadvantages.
- Second solution proposed:
    Advantages and disadvantages.
- Chosen solution:
    Reasons for choice.

6 Present your strategy to the class.

job rotation in Japan

Job rotation schemes move the employee between a variety of tasks or departments. For example, a member of the marketing department is rotated to serve in the marketing department for six months, and the production department for another six months, before returning to sales. Job rotation aims to:

> motivate the employee by making his/her work more interesting.
> give the employee wider experience of the company's operations, perhaps in preparation to promoting him/her to a senior management position.

A What might be the advantages of job rotation?
B What might be the disadvantages?
C Is job rotation more likely to appeal in a culture whose members have
> HIGH needs to avoid uncertainty?
> LOW needs to avoid uncertainty?
> Check your answer with Hofstede's model, summarized in the Appendix.
D Why might these situations persuade the company NOT to rotate its employees?
> members of the culture prefer specialist careers to generalist careers.
> the company cannot afford the costs incurred by mistakes in production.
> status differences between jobs are treated as very important.
> membership of a group, and loyalty to that group, is very important.
> the costs of training are high.
E Check your answers to d. Which of these explain resistance to job rotation in terms of national culture? Which of these explain resistance in terms of factors other than national culture?

Discuss your answers with other members of the class.

Paddy Ridley, the Australian management consultant, was attending an international conference on New Japanese Business – the Years Ahead. During a lunch break he left the main conference area for lunch in a self-service canteen. There he fell into conversation with two Japanese women managers, both delegates at the same conference. Kumiko Imai was an experienced manager, in her mid-forties. Masako Fukayama was about ten years younger. The topic moved to job rotation as a technique for motivating employees.

Ridley:	Many Asian cultures don't like job rotation.
Fukayama:	Some Japanese people don't like it. But we have to do it.
Imai:	Japanese managers want to be loyal to their company.
Ridley:	Why is loyalty an issue?
Fukayama:	Normally we don't change companies. If you join a Japanese company, and then leave, that looks like disloyalty.
Imai:	And nobody else wants to employ you. You might never find another job.
Fukyama:	Not in a respected company.
Imai:	Yes, very difficult if you hope to move to a respected Japanese company.
Fukayama:	A Western company might employ you, if you have the skills they need.
Imai:	Sometimes, yes.
Fukayama:	So most Japanese hope to stay with their company for all their working life.

Ridley drank the last of his coffee and considered their replies.

Ridley:	But that doesn't answer . . . Why is loyalty to the company an issue when it comes to accepting a job rotation?
Imai:	Because you accept the company's plans to train you.
Fukayama:	Of course, many managers welcome the opportunity. Those that don't, well, they have to go along with it. The company expects its managers to learn all aspects of the business. They have to learn all the functions of the company.
Imai:	So they rotate their managers around departments.
Ridley:	Does that mean that Japanese managers are generalists, not specialists?
Imai:	Most are. And still very few go to business school. We learn within the company, and only the skills that the company requires.
Ridley:	So you two ladies have rotated around your companies?

At this point, the two women smiled.

Fukayama:	We described for you the system for men.
Imai:	Almost all Japanese managers are male.
Ridley:	I know that used to be the case. Is it still true?
Imai:	In some industries. Banks, government bodies and public services, manufacturers, insurance.
Fukayama:	Except life insurance, they began hiring women long ago.
Ridley:	How do Japanese women feel about that?
Fukayama:	It was part of the traditional culture that when the woman marries, she stays at home to bring up the children. We still see that is very important work. And then the child learns from school. We think it very important that the child learns Japanese culture in a Japanese school.
Imai:	When I started work young women in offices were called "Christmas cake." That meant they had no market value after 25. Women normally married before the age of 25.

Fukayama: So the company didn't need invest in women managers. It makes no
            sense to train and promote a woman when very soon she may need to
            quit her job.

Ridley thought about this, then asked them if they'd have another coffee. They
accepted, but Imai insisted that she pay.

Ridley: And women accept that?
Fukayama: Of course there is change. We are both married and we are managers.
            Women can see the change.
Imai: The culture belongs to the women as much as to the men. There are
            many older women who prefer life as it was. They don't want the
            changes. They're like the older men.
Ridley: How do the younger men feel? Those new to the labour force?
Fukayama: Most are liberal. Not all.
Ridley: How do Japanese workers feel about reporting to a female manager?
Fukayama: We know we must change. Those Japanese companies that don't make
            changes are no longer competitive. They go out of business.
Imai: The young people accept it. The older workers sometimes find it
            difficult.
Fukayama: My company is progressive. There are more foreign companies work-
            ing in Japan, and we learn from observing them.
Ridley: But still . . .
Fukayama: Yes. Job rotation is practised widely, but usually for men.
Imai: I entered my bank directly from university. There were twenty of us,
            seventeen men and three women. The male graduates were scheduled
            to rotate between departments every six months. And were wel-
            comed in every department. They learned every aspect of the bank
            busineess.
Fukayama: And the women could not rotate.
Imai: I stayed where I was in import financing.
Ridley: For how long?
Imai: For all my career with the bank.
Fukayama: How did you feel about that?
Imai: When I was young I wanted to move. I wanted to know about credit
            analysis, export financing, transfers, personal loans, all the bank busi-
            ness. But I never did. And then the system turned out to be good
            for me.
Ridley: Why?
Imai: I became a specialist. After twenty years I knew more about import
            financing than any Japanese man.
Ridley: So the system worked for you.
Imai: Yes. Those women who do specialize are rewarded. The company likes
            to demonstrate a policy of giving equal opportunities. So I was pro-
            moted, several times, and I have a title as specialist.
Fukayama: But she is privileged.
Imai: Oh yes. Most women of my generation gave up. They were discour-
            aged by the disadvantages. I'm the only one of my intake that survived.
Fukayama: And she left her bank. She found a senior position with a foreign bank.

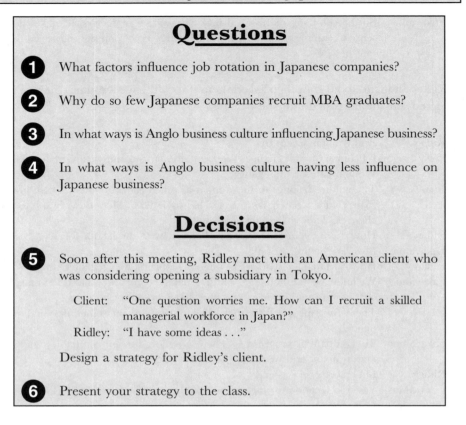

Questions

1   What factors influence job rotation in Japanese companies?

2   Why do so few Japanese companies recruit MBA graduates?

3   In what ways is Anglo business culture influencing Japanese business?

4   In what ways is Anglo business culture having less influence on Japanese business?

Decisions

5   Soon after this meeting, Ridley met with an American client who was considering opening a subsidiary in Tokyo.

> Client: "One question worries me. How can I recruit a skilled managerial workforce in Japan?"
>
> Ridley: "I have some ideas . . ."

Design a strategy for Ridley's client.

6   Present your strategy to the class.

the Anglo–Zambian research and development project

CASE PREPARATION

You are marketing manager in a consumer products company. Your two assistants, Juliet and Hanifa, have different responsibilities which mean that they have to compete for resources. Some conflict is inevitable. They both respect you but are operating below the high standards that you are trying to set. Clearly, they need to be motivated. You tell Juliet that she is your most important assistant and that you entirely depend upon her advice and co-operation. Separately, you are also tell Hanifa that she is your most important assistant and that you entirely depend upon her advice and cooperation.

Answer the following questions:

A In what situations might your policy of deliberate ambiguity be beneficial to your department?
B In what situations might it be damaging?

Discuss your answers with members of the class, and agree how to complete the following:

Deliberate ambiguity is most damaging when ....

....

The original idea had come from two academics meeting at a conference. "A project researching training needs", had enthused the Briton.

"Excellent", agreed the Zambian. "And produce a syllabus and training materials for use in our technical schools."

Each proposed the idea to his sponsoring organization, a Zambian university and a British aid agency, then forgot about it.

In the British agency, the proposal landed on the desk of a senior manager, Tim Yorkshire. Tim had built his highly successful career on developing new projects and this seemed a very good idea. He contacted Professor Gregory Ndolni of the department of education in the Zambian University and they communicated through e-mail and fax. They would cooperate to establish a training project, based in Lusaka and largely funded through British sources. All research staff would be recruited from the British institutions, and all trainers from Zambia. The latter would be given responsibilities of coaching the research staff on the local educational environment.

The Zambians were recruited from the Ministry of Education by Gregory's deputy. They were left in no doubt that their future careers depended on their success in creating development materials.

In London, Tim had expected a foreign posting in about a year. This would have given him plenty of time to confirm plans for the project. But then the German representative was taken ill, and Tim was told to take over in Berlin the next month. He was to be replaced by a subordinate, Maggie Fogg, to whom he handed over his London responsibilities.

The agency encouraged its senior managers to develop their own projects, and Maggie was deeply involved in planning a science project for Indonesia. This was her special interest, and she knew that her career depended on its success. She shuffled impatiently through the paperwork for the Zambian project while Tim explained the details. "Why am I doing this?" she wondered. She resented taking desk responsibilities for someone else's project in which she had no professional interest or stake. If it succeeded Tim would take the credit. If it seemed about to fail she would try to cancel it in a way that did not reflect on her abilities.

"As for project manager," said Tim. "Steve Cussans has a good reputation as a start-up man. He fires interest, creates motivation."

Maggie had never met Steve but knew his reputation. He never stayed longer than a few months in any project, setting up the systems. Strangely, the manager succeeding him usually had to cope with conflicts between project staff and falling morale.

Tim's attention was distracted by a phone call from the Berlin office. Maggie went to a neighboring office to check on Steve's schedule. He was available for the first three months of the two-year project, after which he was booked to start up a similar project in Cambodia.

By the time Tim returned to the topic, she had decided to accept Steve.

"I think that settles it," he said, and in a short time they had sorted out the remaining details.

"Check any queries with Gregory Ndolni," he directed her, "but I think you'll find he's happy to agree."

Maggie used her university connections to recruit a number of academics, all professionally committed to research. They were hired for the duration of the project. She then arranged a meeting with Steve. He was not available on her preferred dates, and she had to reorganize her busy schedule in order to give him time. He had received the project documentation only the previous day, and was still uncertain of the implications.

"What balance should we strike between research and development?" he asked.

"Didn't Tim make that clear?" Maggie looked through the papers, absently. "I'll take up the point with Gregory if you wish. But you're probably better working it out with the staff when you bring them together."

"In other words, muddle through", thought Steve to himself.

Steve flew out to Lusaka two weeks later. He met the staff as they arrived, and initially, they seemed happy to get together. The Zambians had been briefed by Gregory. Steve encouraged a round of parties and dinners in the first few weeks as a way of breaking the ice. Gradually, a routine emerged.

Every Monday morning the full team met and reviewed the project timetable. Steve chaired these meetings. Gregory was always too busy to attend and the research staff only ever met him at social occasions, when he refused to be drawn on project business. However, he maintained regular contact with his Zambian subordinates.

At the meetings plans for the various stages were discussed and sometimes modified in the light of experience to date. Sub-teams described their immediate progress and plans for the week to come. Arrangements for materials production, meetings with outsiders and consultancy visits were discussed and confirmed. Steve encouraged full participation from all, and was unwilling to commit his authority unless certain that a decision was supported by a consensus.

Discussion was open, and ranged far and wide. Decisions once taken could always be reviewed. At one point when a question of organizing consultancy visits was reopened, a researcher complained "we decided that last week".

"Professor Gregory says that the University cannot accept it," a Zambian announced.

"If a mistake has been made, it should be corrected," Steve agreed.

Increasingly, members emerged from these meetings feelings frustrated. After lunch one Monday, the research staff approached Steve in a group.

"These meetings aren't working. They take up too much time and we're going round in circles."

"So what do you suggest we do about it?" Steve asked.

"The problem is, our Zambian friends think they can plan the applications before we've even completed our research. They don't understand the priorities."

"They're not theorists."

"Yes, they can't be blamed for that. But they don't seem to realize that training materials can only be effective when they are based on rigorous research. Too much time is being wasted in pointless discussions."

"I know, I know," interrupted Steve. "I don't like this any more than you do. Believe me, I'm agreed that this is, essentially, a research project. But we are the guests here, and we have to pay lip service to local feelings, even if they are prejudiced."

The researchers left, more or less persuaded that Steve understood and supported their point of view. Steve felt that he had resolved an immediate difficulty. Then, a few days later, he was visited by a delegation of the Zambian trainers.

"We're not happy about the meetings. Every time we try to talk about training issues, the researchers make objections – and never positive. They cannot understand that we have people depending on us. We must produce training materials."

"And we have to spend time explaining about the situation in Lusaka – not that they take any notice."

"We don't need their research," added the most outspoken, Joseph.

"There's plenty of research already available in the literature that we can apply."

Steve said, "They would tell you that it's out of date, and not always relevant to Zambia."

"Yes. But the point is that we can adapt it to our situation. We only need a small element of original research, and we can handle that ourselves. We're not stupid. You should send them all home."

Steve assured them of his full agreement that the main accent of the project was on practical training. He, too, was frustrated by the failure of the researchers to stick to practicalities. However, there could be no question of their being repatriated to the United Kingdom. The British partner was providing the greater part of the funding and had institutional interests in creating new research. The best he could offer was his covert support.

For a short time both sides attempted to work together, but as the weekly meetings became even longer and less productive, patience snapped. The research staff now held their own meetings, and then reporting directly to only Steve. The training staff followed suit. This professional breakdown was accompanied by a collapse in personal relations. The two groups no longer met in social events, and members scarcely acknowledged each other when passing in the corridor.

At this point, Steve received the news that his Cambodian project had been cancelled. He would be managing the Zambian project for the full two years.

In effect though, he was now managing two projects, and the cost to his time was considerable. However, he was satisfied that by being deliberately ambiguous in explaining his strategic goals, he had diffused a potentially explosive situation. For several months the two teams worked productively. The research team analysed a quantity of useful data and were designing an analytical model that had obvious applications. The training team prepared efficient systems by which materials could be written, piloted, revised, and disseminated as widely as possible. By keeping in constant contact with both, Steve was able to ensure a general level of shared information about their different activities. Then, one day, a crisis blew up.

Joseph and one of the researchers met by chance when they were separately invited to a wedding party. After a few drinks they began to discuss the project.

"Of course the focus must be on research," said Michael. "And Steve knows that."

"No, no, Steve wants training material. He told us very strongly."

After a lengthy discussion they separated and began phoning their colleagues. Two days later the two teams came together for the first time in several months, and held a joint meeting – without Steve. The mood was angry. The teams exchanged details of how they had interpreted the project goals. That evening, two of the researchers visited with Steve at home and demanded to be repatriated on contractual grounds – they had expected to be employed in research-led project. The Zambian team met Gregory and demanded that Steve be replaced by one of their own. Eventually, the project was terminated early and very little had been achieved.

Questions

1 In what ways are each of the following responsible for the project failure?
- The two academics who first proposed the project.
- The Zambian university.
- The British aid agency.
- Tim Yorkshire.
- Professor Gregory Ndolni.
- Maggie Fogg.
- Steve Cussans.
- The Zambian staff.
- The British staff.

2 In what respects did the problems in the British aid agency reflect British culture?

3 Why did the discovery made by Michael and Joseph anger the project staff?

4 Defend the policy followed by Steve. Think of circumstances in which this policy might work.

Decisions

5 You are a consultant hired by the British aid agency to evaluate the organizational aspects of is project and to make recommendations for the planning and implementation of similar joint-venture projects.

Your evaluation should take into account (if applicable):
- Failures of this project.
- Responsibility for failures.
- Successes.
- Responsibility for successes.
- Summary of lessons to be learned.
- Recommendations for the planning of future projects.
- Recommendations for the management and implementation of future projects.

6 Present your evaluation and recommendations to the class.

applying American systems in Thailand

CASE PREPARATION

A Review Project 5 (p. 23), which explores the problems of transplanting management systems between cultures.

B Review your understanding of Hofstede's model for comparing cultures, and in particular review the rankings for Thailand and the United States (see the Appendix).

C Select the correct alternative for each of the following:

- in Thailand, power distances are GREATER than / LESS than in the United States.

- in Thailand, needs to avoid uncertainty are GREATER than / LESS than in the United States.

- in Thailand, collectivism is GREATER than / LESS than in the United States.

Dr James Huiston is an expert on the management of higher education and consults to a number of Californian universities. Two years ago he vacationed in Thailand. After energetically visiting the tourist sites of Bangkok and Ayuthya, he spent a few quiet days in a beach hotel. One evening a neighbor in the hotel bar started a conversation. The Thai offered his card; Professor Paron Kamolsak, Director of Administration, Sen Sam University, Bangkok. James remarked on the common ground in their professions, and they spent an interesting evening comparing their situations.

Paron described his university's attempts to modernize.

"Where do you face your greatest difficulties?" James asked.

"Undoubtedly in awarding pay increments and recommending promotions. All faculty receive an automatic rise each year based on tenure. But additional pay awards are made based on performance. There is no general agreement on deciding criteria for who deserves them. In the old system, the Dean of each faculty awarded the faculty who had served him most loyally."

"In other words, patronage. But the ones who weren't rewarded. They must have resented it."

"Of course, they weren't happy. Though if the individual belonged to some other group he might think his time would come around. Or he quit. And at least everybody agreed on the convention."

"And how are promotions awarded?"

Promotions between grades (from lecturer to assistant professor, to associate professor, to full professor) were decided by a university-wide committee, which represented all faculties and departments. This looked only at tenure, teaching excellence and research. The initial pay level in any one grade was higher than the top pay grade in the level below. In practice, the promotions committee usually rubber-stamped proposals made by faculty deans.

Each faculty consists of a number of departments. For example, the Faculty of Science includes departments of physics, chemistry, biology, botany, zoology, mathematics.

Deans and departmental heads are elected every four years. These posts are highly respected and carry a range of privileges, and competition for them is fierce.

"Why do you want to change your reward system?"

"The university wants to plug into international circuits. We need to attract more foreign scholars. To achieve that we need modern systems of rewarding academic staff. Yes, we have to change. We need to engage faculty more openly in the process. But what process? What system should we operate? Getting agreement is not easy."

The evening concluded with Paron inviting James to visit the university the following month in a consulting role and to make a formal report.

"I can arrange interviews with a range of academics and administrators. I have no doubt that they will be happy to give you their views. As an outsider you cannot be identified with any of the competing factions. You will be seen as a neutral."

James sighed. "I'm afraid that's out of the question. I have meetings next month in San Diego. But what I could do is extend by two days now, talk to some of your people and perhaps we might review your options."

Paron's colleagues were as helpful as he had promised, and James enjoyed his short visit to the campus. On the evening before his return to the United States, Paron hosted him at a banquet attended by senior officers of the university. They discussed the options.

"Two days is too short a learning time and I'm not in a position to advise on the details of an incremental system that meets your needs. All I feel able to do is to make general points. I assume that your goals are both to motivate academic standards and to introduce rational bureaucratic standards that improve on the existing state."

The Thais murmured their agreement.

James continued. "From what I've been told, you wish to reward excellence in a range of areas that include research, teaching, administration, committee work and other extracuricular responsibilities. So, in order to qualify for a salary rise or promotion, an academic must excel in the priority areas."

"And which are those? How do we weigh them against each other?"

"That is the point at which I don't feel competent to help. You know your priorities better than I do."

"What would you choose back home?"

"In a research institute, research skills take priority. In a junior college, teaching skills. In most of my situations, most academics would not expect to play a major role in administration."

The Thais fell silent. The problem of agreeing on priorities remained. They were grateful to James for his ideas, but could not see any immediate hopes of implementing them. Certainly the University Rector lacked the political muscle to enforce a controversial system against the wishes of academic staff, who in many cases had powerful connections outside the university.

After James had flown out, a short written report summarizing his general points was circulated by Paron's office. Faculty committees were instructed that they were at liberty to discuss and apply the proposals to their own needs. Provided that substantial support within the faculty could be demonstrated, the university authorities would accept and support the faculty decision. No attempt would be made to enforce a single set of regulations across the university – unless faculty wanted this.

A few months later, Paron was informed that the Faculty of Political Science had decided to implement the proposal. The Faculty consisted of five departments, and had been led for eight years by a highly traditional Dean. He had exercised extensive powers of patronage by awarding his clients double pay rises at will. Only they had received conference trips abroad and promotions to senior grades.

Now a group of aggrieved faculty had forced his retirement and elected their own candidate. They then elected a committee to decide on issues of pay and promotion. Several weeks later the Pay and Promotions Committee made a formal proposal, on which junior faculty were invited to communicate their opinions. They, rather than the Dean, would be responsible for recommending promotions. The criteria for promotions would not change.

In order to qualify for a rise, the member of faculty will need to prove himself or herself in ALL the following activities:

- excellence in teaching
- research
- administration
- committee work
- outside teaching engagements
- other extracuricular responsibilities

Departmental heads will be responsible for awarding places on committees and outside work assignments.

Questions

1 What aspects of this case reflect Hofstede's findings for Thai culture in comparison to American culture (see the Appendix).

(a) What aspects of this case do you think are unlikely to occur in an American university (or a university in any other Anglo culture of which you have experience?) Why?

2 What problems do you expect to arise from the proposed reform? How might the organizational culture contribute to these problems?

Decisions

3 You are a consultant. The university authorities accept your analysis of the expected problems (Question 2 above). They have asked you, as a trusted outsider, to:

(a) propose a policy on promotions and incremental pay rises.

(b) indicate what changes need to be made to the organizational culture in order to facilitate your policy on promotions and pay rises.

Prepare a presentation based on your answers to (a) and (b).

4 Make the presentation.

repatriation

CASE PREPARATION

Suppose that, tomorrow, you have to leave the business school and relocate to a work-study project in a distant country. After two years working abroad you are brought back to the business school in order to complete your studies.

What do you imagine will be the three greatest problems that you experience on re-entry to your country and business school?

A ....

Why will this be a problem? ....

B ....

Why? ....

C ....

Why? ....

Discuss your answers with members of the class.

The consultant Paddy Ridley had been working with a German engineering firm on its organization culture. At his final meeting with the general manager, Heinz-Harald Massagni, he asked about the company's systems for reintroducing its returned expatriates to headquarters.

"How are they affected by changes in the organization culture? How do they contribute to it?"

Heinz-Harald shrugged wearily. "We have had some problems, I can tell you. I'm not able to give an answer. Japanese returnees seem able to settle back to headquarters routines without any serious problems. How do they manage it?"

Paddy suggested: "When the Japanese manager is at post, his career interests are protected in headquarters. He knows what he's returning to."

"Is that confidence reflected in success at the posting? That would make sense. Most of our European and North American postings *are* successful. But our success rates in Africa and Asia are far less rosy. That's true for most European firms. American firms have even greater problems. We are setting up new projects in Thailand, Indonesia and Vietnam. Over the next ten years we expect to expatriate a number of engineers and managers to all these countries, some for a few months and some for a couple of years. What sort of repatriation problems should we expect? What can we do to prevent them, or resolve them?"

A few hours later Paddy was waiting in the business class lounge of the airport when he unexpectedly met a Japanese acquaintance, waiting for the same flight. Hiroshi politely enquired about how he liked Frankfurt, and for a few minutes they exchanged notes on the city's many excellent restaurants. Then Paddy mentioned his current work on organization culture, and moved the topic to repatriation.

"For many business people the problems are both professional and personal. Reduced financial benefits, alienation from headquarters staff."

"Yes, I know what can happen in an Anglo company, particularly where turnover is high. The expatriate returns to find that his old headquarters friends have left or been posted and there's no one around that he can put a name to."

"I have a client who is interested in Japanese experiences. And how the company can ease the adjustment."

Hiroshi said, "Sometimes the spouse suffers more than the manager. When that happens, how can the company help?"

Then he told a story of a Japanese manager, employed by a major Japanese trading company with branches across the world.

Kanji was about 27 years old when he was posted to his company's office in Jakarta. He was accompanied by his wife, Sumiko, and their children aged five and two. Repatriation had been a shock.

"How did he respond?"

"Not for him. He was neither happy nor unhappy. He had known that they would be kept in post for six years, then repatriated. At post the company trained him for re-entry. Sumiko was the one to suffer."

Ridley thought about this and said "Accommodation."

"In part. Their accommodation was allocated by the company. Under the SHATAKU system, the company finds accommodation. In a town like Jakarta, company managers were scattered."

"So far as I remember, Jakarta has few apartments."

"Yes. And expatriate managers typically live in large houses. There had planty of space, far more than a manager could expect in Japan. There were rooms for a maid, and of course on his salary they could afford one."

"On his salary?"

Hiroshi corrected himself. "Strictly speaking, on his expatriate allowance, in Indonesia paid in US dollars. He had been a sales rep in Osaka, then made a section manager in Jakarta. But that a sideways move, no promotion. Back home in Osaka, a sales rep again. He had expected that before he left."

"But of course his Japanese salary went further in Jakarta."

"Much further. Living costs are far less in Indonesia than Japan."

"So they enjoyed the life."

"They had a good social life. They went out together far more often than at home. She spoke good English and Chinese, and started learning Indonesian. She made a wide circle of friends among the other expatriate communities and among Indonesian women too. She joined local clubs. She joined an American theatre club."

"How did the other wives respond to that?"

Hiroshi laughed. "Exactly. That contributed to the problem. As you know, the wives of managers belong to the company wives' club. The club manages their social activities, and most Japanese wives are happy to stick together. Typically, they have no dealings with local people. Indonesian culture is perceived as distant from Japanese."

"Added to that, the hierarchy of the club is strict. It reflects the hierarchy of their husband's posts. In an expatriate setting, the wife of the chief executive officer is a very powerful lady."

"But Sumiko did not fit in?"

"She had as little to do with the wives' club as possible. She made herself very unpopular. In Jakarta that did not bother her."

"But when they returned home?" Paddy asked.

"Exactly. She had made many enemies, and back in Osaka could not escape the jealousies. She got into several shouting matches. She fell out with even her friends. She desperately needed to talk about her experiences and nobody would listen. The attitude was 'Now you're back home you must fit in.' And the children suffered. In school they were stigmatized as different, and they were seriously bullied."

"So what happened?"

"It was a sad case. Kanji was increasingly upset by her behavior, and his job performance deteriorated. He felt a stronger loyalty to the company and he left her. Sumiko broke down completely and was admitted to a mental hospital."

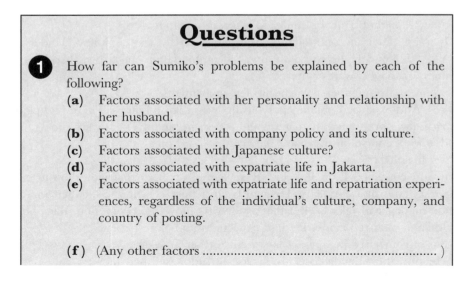

Questions

1 How far can Sumiko's problems be explained by each of the following?

(a) Factors associated with her personality and relationship with her husband.

(b) Factors associated with company policy and its culture.

(c) Factors associated with Japanese culture?

(d) Factors associated with expatriate life in Jakarta.

(e) Factors associated with expatriate life and repatriation experiences, regardless of the individual's culture, company, and country of posting.

(f) (Any other factors ....)

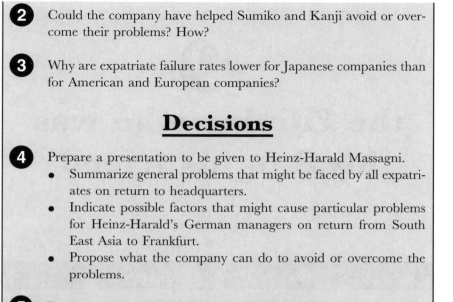

2 Could the company have helped Sumiko and Kanji avoid or overcome their problems? How?

3 Why are expatriate failure rates lower for Japanese companies than for American and European companies?

Decisions

4 Prepare a presentation to be given to Heinz-Harald Massagni.
- Summarize general problems that might be faced by all expatriates on return to headquarters.
- Indicate possible factors that might cause particular problems for Heinz-Harald's German managers on return from South East Asia to Frankfurt.
- Propose what the company can do to avoid or overcome the problems.

5 Present your analysis and proposals to the class.

the Filipino who was loyal to his friend

CASE PREPARATION

Most companies reward loyalty by their employees, and punish disloyalty. Most companies reward honesty and punish dishonesty. But is loyalty always a virtue? Is dishonesty always a vice?

Try to think of situations in your culture when:

A The company might punish your loyalty to other members.

B The company might reward disloyalty.

C The company might reward dishonesty.

Discuss your answers with other members of the class who come from other cultures.

- Do all cultures interpret the notion of loyalty in the same way?
- Do all cultures interpret the notion of honesty in the same way?

Explain any differences.

A senior Filipino executive of an American subsidiary based in Metro Manila and an American executive from the Chicago headquarters together interviewed a Filipino seeking promotion from payroll assistant manager to payroll manager.

When they came to the dimension of "integrity" the interviewers asked "Everyone has to bend or break the rules sometime. Can you give an example of when you had to do this?"

The candidate, Felix, had never broken any major company rules.

"But . . . ," he hesitated.

"But what?" the American demanded.

"I once helped Jaime."

He explained that Jaime, a member of his work group, had asked him to issue a letter certifying his salary at a higher level than was true.

"Why did he ask for that?"

"So he could qualify for a bank loan. I thought it over carefully and asked my wife. Then I decided that I could not deny Jaime. He is a close friend, and at the time he was having serious difficulties. His child was ill and needed hospital treatment. And he had to make repairs to his house. Also, I knew that if Jaime did not get the loan many people would think that he had been badly treated. Other people in the work group would become angry. The work group would become impossible to manage."

Felix had calculated Jaime's salary at a figure that included bonus and other allowances, and certified this as the basic salary.

When Felix had left the room, the two interviewers discussed their ratings. The Filipino had rated Felix as acceptable on the dimension of integrity.

"Why?" queried the American, surprised.

"Because I like his sensitivity to his friend's need. Also, he considered the harmony of the work group."

"Only because he was frightened of unpopularity. But a good manager must expect to be unpopular at some times – perhaps all the time."

"Perhaps. But he is certainly correct that productivity would have suffered. No. I don't consider the subterfuge to be serious. After all, Jaime repaid the loan to the bank. No one suffered."

The American disagreed. "Felix knew the company rules and he should have denied the request. Company rules apply to everyone, regardless of rank. They apply equally to you and me. The company cannot make exceptions. Felix has not given a good reason for his behavior. He was weak."

"But he felt strong enough to admit to the incident."

"That is not the point. His integrity cannot be trusted."

The differences between the interviewers were only resolved when the American washed his hands of the process, insisting that he make a written report of his objection to the promotion and that his Filipino colleague take responsibility for any problems that might arise from making it.

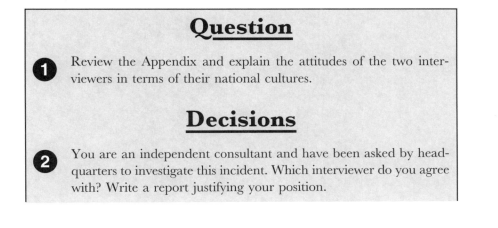

Question

1 Review the Appendix and explain the attitudes of the two interviewers in terms of their national cultures.

Decisions

2 You are an independent consultant and have been asked by headquarters to investigate this incident. Which interviewer do you agree with? Write a report justifying your position.

3 Debate with other members of the class. Justify your position to persons who have taken an opposite position. Which of the following explains your differences?

- cultural difference
- gender difference
- ethical differences
- any other differences

Afolayan Supplies

CASE PREPARATION

The structure of an organization organizes its members and the units in which they are clustered. It regulates their responsibilities for work, and their relationships with each other.

Answer the following questions:

A Think of three situations in which the company may decide to change its structure.

B Think of three situations in which the company may decide NOT to change its structure – even though the business environment has changed.

Discuss your answers with other members of the class.

Thirty years ago, George Afolayan established an office supplies company in Lagos, Nigeria. Afolayan Supplies developed a profitable niche in supplying Nigeria's new state industries and the various international agencies represented in the capital. Over the years, the company flourished. It succeeded because of energetic marketing in the early years, and a continuing reputation for making deliveries on schedule.

George's eldest son died in a motoring accident several years ago. His eldest daughter moved abroad with her husband, a diplomat. The second daughter is a successful academic and has no interest in entering business. George's second son and eldest surviving child, Freddie, was the only one in the family who had shown any interest in a business career. He had worked part-time in the company since his school days and it had always been understood that when he completed his business study he would move into management in the family firm.

That move was now close. Freddie was about to graduate with an MBA from a prestigious European business school when he received an e-mail from his father. The old man was making a business trip, visiting suppliers. He arranged to meet his son at the comfortable London hotel where he usually stayed.

When they met, Freddie politely enquired about his father's health. His father thanked him. After a moment's silence he began to speak with an urgency that his son had seldom heard before.

"Freddie my son, I am now an old man. Yes, yes I am. The business is a great strain, and I want to pass it on to you as soon as I can. I want to free myself from it, altogether. This is difficult for you. You have not yet graduated, and are not fully prepared. However, there is no alternative. I am appointing you General Manager, reporting only to me, but in practice you will be taking the decisions. You know the business well and I shall be always there to give you advice. And of course, there are others who can help – your uncle, Wole, but of course he is close to retirement, and he is not a well man. There is Sonny, and he is closer to your age. I have great hopes for him, and have decided to promote him. He is like a second son to me, and you will please me by treating him as your brother."

Freddie heard this with mixed feelings. Sonny Ekun was about three years the older, and when they had been boys together, had always tried to impose his own views and opinions. He was the son of George's old friend, now deceased. When Sonny Senior was on his death bed, George had promised to look after Sonny Junior and take him into the firm. Soon after Freddie's departure for Europe, Sonny had been appointed to a vacant position as Assistant Production Manager. He had charm and a good business brain, but Freddie was not sure that he wanted him so close to the heart of the company.

The company was structured along the line of figure 20.1.

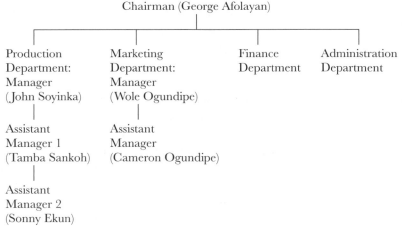

● **Figure 20.1**

It had very soon become clear that Sonny should not have been appointed to the Production Department. First, he showed no great interest in production. He was usually late for work and left early. He had inherited considerable wealth from his father, and enjoyed socializing. Second, a personality conflict arose between Sonny and the other Production Assistant Manager, Tamba Sankoh. Tamba was a conscientious and efficient worker. He was respected, but had no close friends.

He disliked socializing and found it difficult to respond to his more extroverted colleague. Further, he greatly resented the other's constant absenteeism and how this affected his own work load.

The total work load for the Production Department seemed likely to grow. Local supply problems meant that increasing quantities of timber would have to be imported from abroad. How far this situation might continue was still anyone's guess, but John Soyinka had agreed that his department would take on purchasing responsibilities for at least the short term. Most of the extra work had fallen on Tamba's desk.

The effects of Sonny's activities were not entirely negative. His network of friends was extensive, and included the sons of many wealthy families. These social connections were responsible for the firm landing several contracts that it could not have otherwise expected.

Unfortunately, there was no post available within the Marketing Department that Sonny was prepared to accept. Wole Ogundipe had recently appointed his son Cameron as his Assistant, but this injection of new blood had done nothing to dispel the sense of decay that hung over the department. The order book was still full, thanks to a reputation earned in the past and Sonny's informal activities. But it had been some time since any new items had entered production. George tried suggesting to Wole that the Marketing Department badly needed shaking up and that Sonny might be brought in as a second Assistant Manager, but his brother-in-law responded so angrily that the matter was dropped.

But Sonny had not been prepared to wait. He made clear that he was disappointed by the company and was looking for a move. George was worried, for both personal and business reasons. He was conscious of his promise to Sonny Senior, that he would employ the young man. And there was no doubting the value of Sonny's social connections.

In an effort to get a clearer idea of how Sonny could best contribute to the company, George entertained him to dinner in an expensive restaurant. Sonny quickly relaxed, and began to talk about his interests and ambitions. At university he had taken courses in computing, and was excited by the applications to a family business like Afolayan Furniture. As the waiter removed the sweet plates and they relaxed over a brandy, he said "It seems to me we could really profit if we developed a Computer Center." He took out a pen and began to list its functions on the back of a menu.

Next day in the office, George and Sonny met again. Plans were made to set up the new Center very much along the lines that Sonny had suggested, and with himself as manager. Broad guidelines were set for capital expenditure. George congratulated himself that he had separated Sonny and Tamba, thus resolving the problem of conflict between them, and in a way that found a useful occupation for Sonny.

The development went rapidly ahead. George was taken seriously aback by the outlay on hardware, but Sonny reassured him, "with a capacity like this, I'm certain we can get contract work from the external market. Don't worry, we'll very soon start paying for ourselves. The Computer Center is going to be a major profit center."

This was the point at which Freddie returned from studying. As promised, he was appointed General Manager. He had been given no warning of his father's decision to establish the Computer Center. The company now looked different (figure 20.2).

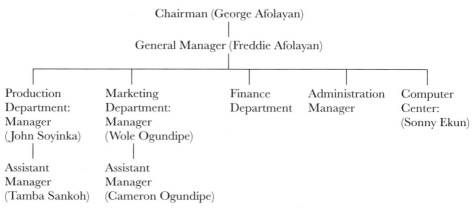

Chairman (George Afolayan)

General Manager (Freddie Afolayan)

Production Department: Manager (John Soyinka)

Marketing Department: Manager (Wole Ogundipe)

Finance Department

Administration Manager

Computer Center: (Sonny Ekun)

Assistant Manager (Tamba Sankoh)

Assistant Manager (Cameron Ogundipe)

Figure 20.2

Over the next few weeks, it became clear that the new Computer Center was underemployed. The three persons recruited by Sonny had time on their hands. Freddie was all the more surprised, then, to learn that Sonny had approached George about employing a new secretary, and that George had immediately agreed. The first that Freddie had learned about it was when he discovered the young woman sitting in Sonny's office.

He could not disguise his irritation when he spoke to his father. "How can I exercise authority if hirings are made without my knowledge, let alone without my permission?"

"I hope you don't forget that I am still the Chairman," growled the old man, equally angry. "And that means I take the decisions."

Freddie was forced to accept the situation. He tried talking to Sonny about resourcing demands which seemed to him far too high considering that the unit's most obvious activity each month was computing the company payroll. But Sonny laughed, and said he was surprised that a top-school MBA was unable to appreciate the values of investing in information technology.

"It's the latest technology. Everybody wants to do business with a company that is up to date. It's our having the technology that matters, not my staff and how they spend their time." "The bubble will burst quickly enough if they can't do anything." "It's your father I owe my job to, not to you – whatever your title." And Sonny left the office, slamming the door.

Freddie reflected that their relationship seemed to have deteriorated since his return from Europe. Sonny himself had never had a chance to study abroad, and this may have increased his resentment at having to take direction from the better-educated younger man whom he had previously treated as his junior.

That evening he called round to have dinner in his parent's house. As they sat out on the verandah enjoying a beer, George remarked, "Sonny tells me that you're worried about our investment. And about his plans to start developing software."

"Software? He never mentioned that. What software is this?"

"For setting up transportation systems. The way that Lagos traffic is building up, there's bound to be a market. I've been over the figures with him, and he's convinced me. Of course, it's going to mean some retraining, and restructuring."

"We seem to be changing the structure in order to accommodate the interests of just one person," said Freddie, trying to master his temper.

"This is not a problem in your business school," said George.

"This is Africa. And I am still your father."

A further problem blew up the next day. Freddie was touring the factory when Tamba Sankoh approached him. "I can't accept this situation," he said. "I've lost too much face. I'm quitting Friday."

"What's happened now?"

"I'm not working any longer in the same company as Sonny."

Freddie was astounded. It had seemed that the one great benefit of giving Sonny his own unit was that he and Tamba were separated. "He's been promoted, hasn't he?" explained Tamba, "Things were bad enough when we were both Assistant Managers. But now he's been given his own department and I haven't moved. People are laughing at me. I've lost face with everyone. So I'm quitting."

"No, don't make any definite decision yet. Let me sort this out," said Freddie.

Reluctantly, Tamba agreed, but on the understanding that if no solution had been found by the end of the month, he would go.

Freddie was very unwilling to let Tamba go. Afolayan Furniture could only hope to survive the immediate future if the production department maintained its high morale and performance. Moreover, Tamba was developing a purchasing expertise that promised to greatly benefit the company in the future.

When Freddie spoke to George that evening, he was surprised to find his father unmoved. "Let him go if he wants to. We don't owe him anything. I know that he works well. But we don't know anything about him. We can never fully trust him. I can't understand his Ibu, and even his English is peculiar. He's not even a proper Nigerian."

This was true. Tamba's parents had emigrated from elsewhere in West Africa.

"And he still doesn't have the experience. I can't consider him for promotion."

Freddie restrained himself from pointing out that he, too, had lacked top management experience a few months before when he had returned with his new MBA and been immediately appointed General Manager. "If he goes on the labor market, someone's going to hire him for more than we pay. We'll be the losers."

George shrugged. "Well, you're running the company now. This is your decision."

Questions

1   Who is in dispute with whom? Over what issues?

2   How far was the decision to change the structure justified? How far was it unjustified?

3   What problems face Freddie? What factors have caused these problems? How far are cultural factors a cause?

Decisions

4   You are a consultant. You have been hired to propose solutions to the problems analyzed above. For each problem propose a solution.

5   Suggest procedures by which your solutions (proposed in Question 3) can be implemented.

6   What further problems might arise in the future from implementing your solutions?

7   Prepare a presentation explaining your:

     analysis of problems
     proposed solutions
     proposed implementation procedures
     analysis of further possible problems

8   Present your analysis and proposals to the class.

when to keep quiet

CASE PREPARATION

Review recent discussions with:

- Your teacher.
- Some other professional person (for instance, a bank manager, a physician).
- A friend.

Answer the following questions:

A In each discussion, what were your goals? What were you trying to achieve?

B In each were you successful or unsuccessful in achieving these goals?

C What factors influenced your success or failure?

Discuss your answers with other members of the class.

Paddy Ridley, the Australian management consultant, was in Seoul completing a contract for a local engineering company. A banquet had been arranged, at which Paddy and a number of expatriate colleagues were entertained by key members of the company. At the end of the banquet, a number of the guests switched places, and Paddy found himself a seat next to a younger member of the staff with whom he had not spoken before.

Kim was happy to talk about himself. After completing a degree at the National University of Korea he had worked for six years in a local company, then gone to the United States to take an MBA degree at a prominent mid-west business school.

"Did you enjoy that?" Paddy asked.

The Korean smiled and said "It was difficult at first."

"Perhaps you found the food unusual?"

"Not the food. Knowing when to talk." And when Paddy looked surprised, he continued. "In Korea, a university student keeps his mouth shut in lectures. You only hear one person talking. The professor is the most important person in the classroom and he's the expert. He has the experience, and he's read the books. The students are there to learn. They don't have the experience."

"So they don't contribute?"

"If the professor asks you a question, of course. Or if you have particular experience, but that's unusual."

"And suppose you don't agree with something he says?"

"You keep quiet. You think perhaps you're wrong. The professor must know. No student is going to open his mouth to disagree, whatever he might think."

"Why not?"

"Because that sounds like a challenge. That challenges the professor's authority. That makes everybody unhappy."

"But can't you ask a question?"

"That might sound like a criticism, as though the professor had failed to explain himself properly the first time."

"And what happened when you went to the American business school?"

"I was shocked. I and my Korean friends. We sat in the front row of the class to hear everything the professors said. But the American students talked all the time. They asked questions. They gave their own ideas."

"So what did you think?"

"We thought they must be very experienced. They seemed to know everything. We thought that we can never compete with these people."

"And sometimes a student disagreed with the professor. Once the professor made a mistake writing a formula on the board, and the American students told him. We were embarrassed for him. We could not understand why he did not expel them from the class."

"So what happened then?"

"We thought that perhaps we could learn from the American students. We listened carefully to what they said. We made notes."

"And then?"

"We began to realize that a lot of the time the students didn't know much. Often they were wrong, or were talking about things that had nothing to do with what the professor had said."

"So you lost your respect for your colleagues?"

"Not entirely. Some of them were very clever, some less so. That's the same in every class, in the United States, in Korea, in every country. But we began to think that the talking meant something different in Korea and the United States."

"How do you mean – what were the American students doing by talking?"

"First, a student has to say something to show that he – or she – is there. Then they must show they are participating. This can mean contributing your own experience, or giving an opinion. Arguing isn't bad as it might be in Korea. Arguing can be creative."

"So you came to think that too? And you began to argue with the Professor?"

Kim smiled. "I guess that old habits are difficult to break. We're taught to show respect to professors, so most of the time we kept quiet. But we weren't so worried by the other students any longer."

"And when you graduated?"

"I worked in a Chicago company for a few years."

"And then you returned to Korea?"

The party was breaking up, and they were interrupted by another of the guests. Paddy did not get an answer to his question – for several months. Then, one day when he was back in Seoul working with another company, he took a call in his hotel room. Kim was in reception, and wondered if they might talk for a few minutes. Paddy was delighted to be back in contact with his friend, and went down to meet him in the bar.

Kim remembered very well the point at which they had broken off their last conversation. "The difficulties began when I returned home. The difficulties for me. I have decided to change my job. In Korea that is not so easy. But my present situation is becoming impossible."

"Why impossible?"

"Perhaps I learned the American style too well. I was no longer very good at listening to what my superiors told me when I thought they were talking nonsense."

"Can you give an example?"

"You know my company. It's family owned. Mr Park is a nice man and when we manufactured air conditioners, he knew the technology well and made all the decisions."

"That was before I met him."

"Yes, times have changed. Now we manufacture hospital equipment. This is project work. We design a piece of equipment for this hospital, manufacture and install it, then train the technicians. And the next client probably needs something quite different. Mr Park no longer understands the technologies. Well, so many technologies are involved that no one person can be the only expert. And although it was his decision, he doesn't understand this way of doing business. Project work means consulting internally, continuously, with people from marketing, R&D, finance, so on. All can make inputs to the project."

"So where is the difficulty?"

"Mr Park can't change his management style. He wants to make all the decisions. He doesn't like to ask for information about things he doesn't understand. He is frightened of losing face. So I become frustrated. I cannot contribute."

Paddy began to think about those western companies operating in Korea that would be happy to employ a skilled engineer like Kim.

Questions

1 Review Hofstede's model in the Appendix. How far does this explain Kim's experiences?

2 "In order to be persuasive, a communications must be appropriate to its context." How far is this illustrated by Kim's experiences in the American business school? Back in the Korean company?

Decisions

3 An international consulting company is contracting you to write an analysis of the organizational factors in traditional cultures that inhibit rapid economic growth. Use the material above.

4 Present your analysis to the class.

part II

projects

comparing cultures

AIM: This project gives practice in analysing and comparing cultures.*

Specifically, Project 1 asks you to:

- Complete a short questionnaire.
- Conduct the questionnaire among members of two different culture groups.
- Analyze the findings.
- Compare the cultures.
- Prepare a presentation reporting the findings.
- Present.

Instructions

1 Check your understanding of:
The Appendix
Case 1

2 Read the seven questionnaire items below. Which one of Hofstede's dimensions are they asking about?

Questionnaire (A–G)

A Suppose that your teacher announces today that he will give you a short surprise test sometime in the next few days. Do you feel:

very high anxiety	high anxiety			low anxiety	almost no anxiety
a	b	c	d	e	f

---

* Note: this project can only be conducted when the class has access to members of more than one national culture.

B Your teacher announces that you must leave your present study group and join a new study group. You don't know any of the members of this new group. Do you feel:

very high anxiety	high anxiety		low anxiety	almost no anxiety
a	b	c	d	e	f

C You ask your teacher a question and he/she replies "I don't know. What do you think?" This reply makes you feel:

very com-fortable	com-fortable		uncom-fortable	very uncom-fortable
a	b	c	d	e	f

D Your teachers wish to impose new rules on class attendance, dates for handing in assignments, and examination procedures. This new emphasis on rules makes you feel:

very uncom-fortable	uncom-fortable		com-fortable	very com-fortable
a	b	c	d	e	f

E One of your fellow students loses his temper with the teacher and challenges him openly in class. This makes you feel:

very uncom-fortable	uncom-fortable		com-fortable	very com-fortable
a	b	c	d	e	f

F Usually, your teacher asks you to read a chapter from a textbook in preparation for each class. Today, he gives you a copy of a short story, which he says illustrates the teaching point better than any textbook. This innovation makes you feel:

very com-fortable	com-fortable		uncom-fortable	very uncom-fortable
a	b	c	d	e	f

G In class, your teacher invites wide open-ended discussion of a topic and seems more concerned with the quality of the discussion than with whether the contributors are right or wrong. This makes you feel:

very com-fortable	com-fortable		uncom-fortable	very uncom-fortable
a	b	c	d	e	f

3 Conduct questions A–G among members of TWO different national cultures. So far as possible:

- Select cultures that are represented among students in your school. The questions refer to student activities, and your findings will have less validity if the respondents are not students.
- Select cultures that are widely separated on this dimension. You would have difficulty justifying your findings if your two groups consisted of, say, respondents from the UK and US.
- Select cultures that are widely represented. The more respondents you can find, the greater the validity of your findings.

4 Score your respondents' answers for questions A–G as follows:
(1) a = 6; b = 5; c = 4; d = 3; e = 2; f = 1
(2) a = 6; b = 5; c = 4; d = 3; e = 2; f = 1
(3) a = 1; b = 2; c = 3; d = 4; e = 5; f = 6
(4) a = 1; b = 2; c = 3; d = 4; e = 5; f = 6
(5) a = 6; b = 5; c = 4; d = 3; e = 2; f = 1
(6) a = 1; b = 2; c = 3; d = 4; e = 5; f = 6
(7) a = 1; b = 2; c = 3; d = 4; e = 5; f = 6

5 You would expect cultures that score in the region 32–42 to be ranked at the high end of the dimension. You would expect cultures that score in the region 7–17 to be ranked at the low end of the dimension. Check with Hofstede's model (see the Appendix).

6 For each of the two national cultures, what do your findings say about the culture group?

....

....

Do your findings agree with Hofstede?
YES/NO
If NO, why not? What special features do your respondent group have that means they are not typical of their national culture?

....

....

....

7 Now write three new questionnaire items (H–J). Develop these from Hofstede's model as described in the Appendix, applying the same dimension. Write questions that will further reinforce your findings for questions A–G.

Questionnaire (H–J)

H (...
....
....)

    a   b   c   d   e   f

I (...
....
....)

    a   b   c   d   e   f

J (...
....
....)

    a   b   c   d   e   f

8 Conduct questions H–J among the same members of the same two national cultures interviewed in 3 above.

9 Score your findings to questions H–J. For each of the two national cultures, do they agree with your findings for questions A–G?
YES/NO
If NO, why not?
Do they agree with Hofstede's findings?
YES/NO
If NO, why not?

10 Using your findings analysed in Instructions 6 and 9, predict how members of each of these two groups of respondents might behave in the following situations.
- Applying for a job.
- Accepting suggestions from a subordinate.
- Accepting suggestions from a superior.
- Working on a project that may have no clear outcome.
- Dealing with a subordinate who regularly arrives a few minutes late for work.

What further predictions can you make?

11 Use the information that you have collected above to prepare a presentation. This reports on:
- Your identification of Hofstede's dimension (Instruction 2 above).
- Your selection of culture groups (Instruction 3 above).
- The scores made by each culture group for questions A–G (Instruction 2 above).

- Your analysis of the scores for questions H–J (Instruction 6 above).
- Your new questions H–J (Instruction 7 above).
- Your revised findings (Instruction 9 above).
- Your predictions of behavior (Instruction 10 above).
- Any suggestions as to how Hofstede's model can be further applied?

12 Make the presentation.

designing a
management study
skills course

AIM: This project gives practice in designing a training course.

Specifically, Project 2 asks you to:

- Analyze data.
- Identify priorities.
- Design a training course.
- Prepare a presentation.
- Present.

Instructions

1 Read and discuss this case material about the Kingston-American Business Academy (KABA).

2 Design a training course that meets KABA's needs, and also promises to motivate the students. So far as you can, use the ideas given in the case material.

3 Prepare to present your design to the class.

4 Present.

David works for the Kingston-American Business Academy (KABA). KABA offers a two-year international MBA programme in the medium of English. He is a communications expert and at present teaches academic study skills including reading, note-taking, lecture comprehension, and presentation to new students who lack these essential skills.

Students recommended for these classes have to take them in addition to their regular MBA classes during teaching semesters. Many come from countries in which English is not the first language, and so they find it difficult to work at the same pace as the native English speakers.

This situation led to work-load problems. Students who did not have time to complete their reading and writing assignments were under severe strain, and the number failing examinations and dropping out from the school rose significantly.

The Dean, Don Carter, decided to end this teaching of academic skills at the same time as the MBA courses. He plans to replace it with a sixteen-week Graduate Foundation Programme (GFP) that will be offered to all students before embarking on MBA studies. Students who lack poor language and study skills will only be accepted for the MBA programme when they have completed GFP. GFP will also be made available to students wishing to proceed to graduate study in other institutions.

David has been asked to propose a GFP that teaches in three main areas:

- remedial language
- study skills
- introductory business

David invited an old friend to visit the school and to help him plan the proposal. If the proposal was accepted, he hoped to employ her in the GFP teaching team. Alice was an expert on teaching pre-MBA level management and developing student projects.

First he showed her around the school; the lecture theatres, classrooms, the technology rooms, the library. Then they joined Don Carter to eat lunch in the faculty canteen. Alice was impressed by standard of food and service.

Alice: "How far does the School subsidize the canteen?"
David: "This is an independent operation. The School has a policy of contracting out services when it can. The campus also has student canteens, a book shop, a sports wear shop, a drug store, and a cinema all of which operate as independent profit centers. The School subsidizes their utilities, which keeps the prices down."
Alice: "What profit margins do they operate on? How do they market to your international students? Who do they recruit and what employment policies do they follow?"
David: (laughing) "The questions are interesting but I can't tell you. It shouldn't be difficult to find out. The managers are all friendly people who welcome suggestions."

The conversation moved on to other topics but David could see that Don had been impressed by her interest in how the School functioned.

Alice: "What do we know about these students? How are their language standards?"
David: "Varied. All have passed the ABC language test, which we use as a basic testing instrument. But some scraped through and they need more work. Some are comfortable."

Alice: "And what about prior experience?"
David: "Varied again. Some have completed first degrees in business."
Don: "So we focus on designing classroom materials that translate these basic ideas into English."
David: "Only for a few students. Many have qualifications in quite different fields. This year we have a Korean student whose first degree is music. Some have done MBAs in their own countries. All have some experience of working but not all have worked in management."
Don: "So we have to devise a programme for a class that includes these students."

He had been writing a list of the different student groups and he showed it to them.

- local MBAs
- first degrees (in English or some other language) in business-related subjects
- first degrees (in English or some other language) in subjects entirely unrelated to business
- students who have management experience
- students who have no management experience.

David: "In general, yes. But the management experience, no management experience, distinction is not clear-cut. Some have performed management roles but without taking formal titles."
Don: "Why not?"
Alice: "What titles are we talking about?"
Don: "Like Assistant Marketing Manager, Head of the Computer Section, so on."
David: "Exactly. Many of the foreign students have worked in their family companies for years. They do every job that comes along, including managing the non-family labour."
Don: "With no formal job titles. But . . ."
Don: "And they don't specialize."
David: "For example, we have one Taiwanese student in her early twenties who's worked in the family hardware store since she was ten. At first she fetched snacks for the workforce and cleaned. Then she stacked shelves and listed inventory. Then she was moved on to doing accounts and managing some of the sales operations."
Alice: "When did she have the time?"
David: "Evenings and weekends when she had finished her school assignments. School and university vacations. The point is that she has immense experience of the work place, but has never had an official title. She always reported to her father."
Alice: "The problem is clear enough. We have to design a programme that holds the attention of students with very different experiences, and that's going to be difficult when they come from different backgrounds."
David: "Exactly. On the one hand we don't want to bore anybody by teaching introductory material they already know. On the other we don't want to talk above anybody's head by assuming that they have experience which they don't."

Alice: "And that's going to make it very difficult to base the program on a set of formal lectures."

David: "What does formal mean here?"

Don: "Say we have a class on introductory accounting. How does the teacher organize the content so it's interesting for those who already have experience and those who might know nothing at all?"

Alice: "Let's change the role of the teacher. And let's say we use the experienced students to teach the inexperienced."

David: "Say, based on project activities."

Alice: "We need projects that are as realistic as possible. We need to put the students into the roles of consultants. Would the School accept student consultants for entry to the MBA program?"

Don: "They would have to demonstrate a mastery of the necessary communication skills. And also that they understand the management principles that underlie their analysis."

David: "I don't think Alice means that we neglect classroom teaching in the subject areas?"

Alice: "No I certainly don't. But whatever teaching we do needs to be integrated with the activities."

David: "Also, we have problems of deciding how to integrate the remedial language and study skills teaching."

Alice: "For example, the students implement a project, study the language necessary to describe it then give a presentation of their findings."

Don: (Laughing) "This is radical talk. You have to come up with some concrete proposals if I'm going to have a hope of convincing the board."

project

3

making real change

AIM: This project gives practice in identifying a real-life problem, formulating a
solution, and (if possible), implementing the solution.

Specifically, Project 3 asks you to:

- Identify a problem in an organization that you know – for example, in your
business school.
- Plan a solution.
- (if appropriate) Implement the solution.
- Complete notes on the above stages.
- Apply the notes in preparing a presentation.
- Present.

Instructions

This project is to be performed in groups of three or four students. All
members of the group are responsible for contributing to the written
material, and only one set of material is required from the group.

Case Writing

1 Each group selects one of the following problems:
(a) a problem of structural relationships within your organization
(within or between units; i.e., groups/departments/divisions/
etc.).
(b) a problem of poor motivation (at any level).
(c) an ongoing conflict within the organization (within or between
units).

WARNING: If you are planning a change for real-life implementation, do not be over-ambitious. For example, you might think of an ideal solution that entails making a new staff appointment or acquiring new premises. But it is highly unlikely that your organization would agree to these steps. Try to find a solution that is practical. For example, in some situations where there is a problem involving structural relationships, you might improve motivation by establishing regular meetings between different units (but at what level?) Your organization might be happy to implement such a change if it seems likely to improve productivity without incurring massive investments.

2 In your group, discuss the problem that you have selected.
- In which department of the organization is this problem chiefly located?

3 Discuss evidence of why and how the problem arises. Collect and analyze relevant data.

4 What further information do you need? How can you obtain that information?

5 Formulate THREE possible solutions. Discuss the advantages and disadvantages of each.

6 Discuss plans for implementing each of the three solutions. For each plan:
- How do members of the organization stand to gain from its implementation?
- Who is most likely to give support?
- Who will be neutral?
- Who will oppose it?
- How can you strengthen your supporters? Move the neutrals to support you? Move the opposers to a neutral position?
- Who among the most senior and influential people in the organization can you enlist to champion this solution?

7 For each plan, what resources do you need in order to implement it (including financial resources, facilities, materials)?

8 For each plan, who can act as agents to implement it?
- What training or preparation do they need?

9 For each plan, to whom should you communicate it?

- For each individual/group to communicate the plan, why does he/she/they need to know?
- For each individual/group, what information needs to be most emphasized?
- For each individual/group, how will you communicate the necessary information?

10 Given your answers to points 6–9, select one of the three plans for implementation.
- Why have you chosen this plan in preference to the others?

11 What problems can you expect in implementing this solution?
- How might these be resolved?

12 How can implementation be monitored?
- By whom?

13 If appropriate, implement your solution.

14 Complete the form given below (Problem Identification, Analysis and Solution).

15 Use the information that you have collected in the form to prepare a presentation. Your presentation must explain each stage of the decisions you made in identifying the problem and planning a solution (points 1–12 above). If appropriate, also explain how you implemented your solution (point 13 above).

16 Make the presentation.

Problem Identification, Analysis and Solution

A   Name of organization: ....

B   Description of problem: ....

....

....

....

C   Unit(s) of the organization in which the problem is located:

....

D Causes of the problem: ....
....
....
....

E Summary of data used to analyse the problem: ....
....
....

F (1) FIRST possible solution: ....
....
....

Advantages of the first possible solution: ....
....
....

Disadvantages of the first possible solution: ....
....
....

(2) SECOND possible solution: ....
....
....

Advantages of the second possible solution:..
....
....

Disadvantages of the second possible solution: ....

....

....

(3)   THIRD possible solution: ....

....

....

Advantages of the third possible solution: ....

....

....

Disadvantages of the third possible solution: ....

....

....

G   (1)   For the FIRST possible solution, how do members of the organization stand to gain from its implementation?

....

....

Who is most likely to give support? ....

Who will be neutral? ....

Who will oppose it? ....

How can you strengthen your supporters? ....

How can you move the neutrals to support you? ....

How can you move the opposers to a neutral position?

....

Who among the most senior and influential people in the organization can you enlist to champion this solution?

....

(2) For the SECOND possible solution, how do members of the organization stand to gain from its implementation?

....

....

Who is most likely to give support? ....

Who will be neutral? ....

Who will oppose it? ....

How can you strengthen your supporters? ....

How can you move the neutrals to support you? ....

How can you move the opposers to a neutral position?

....

Who among the most senior and influential people in the organization can you enlist to champion this solution?

....

(3) For the THIRD possible solution, how do members of the organization stand to gain from its implementation?

....

....

Who is most likely to give support? ....

Who will be neutral? ....

Who will oppose it? ....

How can you strengthen your supporters? ....

How can you move the neutrals to support you? ....

How can you move the opposers to a neutral position?

....

Who among the most senior and influential people in the organization can you enlist to champion this solution?

....

H (1) For the FIRST solution, what resources do you need in order to implement it (including financial resources, facilities, materials)?

....

....

(2) For the SECOND solution, what resources do you need in order to implement it (including financial resources, facilities, materials)?

....

....

(3) For the THIRD solution, what resources do you need in order to implement it (including financial resources, facilities, materials)?

....

....

I (1) For the FIRST solution, who can act as agents to implement it?

....

What training or preparation do they need?

....

(2) For the SECOND solution, who can act as agents to implement it?

....

What training or preparation do they need?

....

(3)   For the THIRD solution, who can act as agents to implement it?

....

What training or preparation do they need?

....

J   (1)   For the FIRST solution, to whom should you communicate the plan?

For each individual/group to communicate the plan, why does he/she/they need to know? ....

....

For each, what information needs to be most emphasized?

....

For each, how will you communicate the necessary information? ......

....

(2)   For the SECOND solution, to whom should you communicate the plan?

For each individual/group to communicate the plan, why does he/she/they need to know? ....

....

For each, what information needs to be most emphasized?

....

For each, how will you communicate the necessary information? ......

....

(3)   For the THIRD solution, to whom should you communicate the plan?

For each individual/group to communicate the plan, why does he/she/they need to know? ....

....

For each, what information needs to be most emphasized?

....

For each, how will you communicate the necessary information? ......

....

K   Which of your three solutions do you choose for implementation? ....

Why have you chosen this plan in preference to the others?

....

L   What problems can you expect in implementing this solution?

....

....

How might these be resolved? ....

M   How can implementation be monitored? ....

....

By whom? ....

spending money

AIM: This project gives practice in formulating a hypothesis and testing it.

Specifically, Project 4 asks you to:

- Evaluate a news story.
- Make a cultural analysis.
- Formulate hypotheses about similar behavior in your own culture.
- Conduct a data survey to test the hypotheses.
- Evaluate the research findings.

INSTRUCTIONS

This story concerns a 36-year-old British businessman, Crispin Odey. Odey worked as a fund manager in the City of London. In 1995, his salary approached £19.25 million. A newspaper commented that:

> the 36-year-old fund manager earned it despite trading losses of £200 million of his clients' money as his golden touch deserted him. . . . Odey doesn't own a car, travels to work in Mayfair by bus [streetcar], shops at Sainsbury's [a supermarket chain] and enjoys Indian takeaways.

> But the Harrow and Oxford-educated businessman owns a £1.5 million house . . ., goes fishing in Scotland and collects fine wines. . . .

> The financier gives an unspecified amount of his salary to a religious group which broke away from the Church of England.*

Odey's wife commented to a second newspaper that he was worth every penny of his salary.

* Laurence Lever, "£20m man who still goes by bus," *The Mail on Sunday*, April 16, 1995.

Nicola Odey, a £100,000-a-year City high-flier herself, said, "Yes, it's a lot of money. But he took a risk setting up his own business. He deserves his success." . . .

The couple, married four years, paid cash for their £1.5 million mansion in London's Chelsea.

But they have none of the other obvious trappings of wealth.

Crispin doesn't own a car, taking the bus to his Mayfair office.

He prefers Indian takeaways and salmon fishing in Scotland to exotic holidays abroad.

"The money gives me a degree of freedom," he says.

The self-made millionaire has his critics.

One former client describes him as "a gambler with other people's money". The ex-client said: "He never made any secret of what he was doing – he never hid anything and there was nothing sinister about what he did."

But referring to last year's losses, the client added: "If he had any respect for other people's money he wouldn't have done what he did."

Crispin accepts criticism as the price of success in Britain.

"People here hate you doing well," he says. "Americans like stories of people doing well, but we don't."*

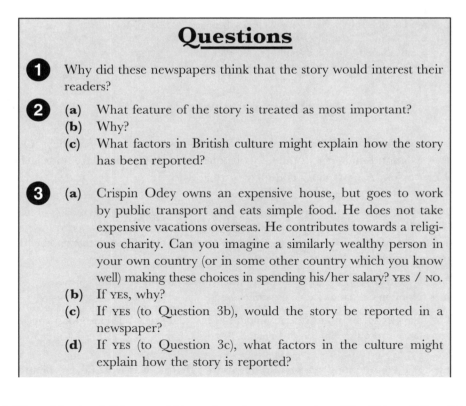

Questions

1   Why did these newspapers think that the story would interest their readers?

2   **(a)**   What feature of the story is treated as most important?
       (b)   Why?
       (c)   What factors in British culture might explain how the story has been reported?

3   **(a)**   Crispin Odey owns an expensive house, but goes to work by public transport and eats simple food. He does not take expensive vacations overseas. He contributes towards a religious charity. Can you imagine a similarly wealthy person in your own country (or in some other country which you know well) making these choices in spending his/her salary? YES / NO.
       (b)   If YES, why?
       (c)   If YES (to Question 3b), would the story be reported in a newspaper?
       (d)   If YES (to Question 3c), what factors in the culture might explain how the story is reported?

* Clinton Manning, "£20m a year? My man's worth every penny (even if he did lose £200m of his clients' money)," *Daily Mirror*, April 17, 1995.

4   If your answer to Question 3a is NO, what different choices might this similarly wealthy person in your own (or in the other country) make?

5   (a)   What factors explain your answer to Question 4?
        (b)   How important are cultural factors?

Project

6   In all cultures, people are interested in how the wealthy use their money, and this is often reported by the media. What topics about wealthy spending do you expect to be most often reported by newspapers in your culture? Here are a few suggestions: examples of wealthy people:

> spending on cheap items.
> refusing to spend on cheap items.
> contributing to charity.
> purchasing property.
> supporting sports.
> giving to the arts.
> supporting education.
> supporting medical research.
> etc.

7   Use your answers to Question 6 to develop hypotheses about newspaper reporting of how the wealthy use their money.

Hypothesis A. NEWSPAPERS REPORT THE WEALTHY USE MONEY ON ...

....

Hypothesis B. NEWSPAPERS REPORT THE WEALTHY USE MONEY ON ...

....

Hypothesis C. NEWSPAPERS REPORT THE WEALTHY USE MONEY ON ...

....

8   Survey as many newspapers as you can find and test your hypotheses. How many items can you find supporting each of your hypotheses?

9 Evaluate the items supporting your hypotheses. Why do you suppose that each story was reported in the press?

(a) Because it is surprising; it contradicts expectations.

(b) Because it is typical; it fulfils expectations.

(c) Because any story about this person is likely to be reported in the newspapers.

(d) Any other reasons?

project

5

transplanting
a management system

AIM: This project gives practice in identifying priorities when transplanting an
management system across cultures – from headquarters to a subsidiary.

Specifically, Project 5 asks you to:

- Read background data on a proposal to transplant a management system.
- Evaluate interview data relating to the proposal.
- Make a cultural analysis.
- Evaluate the likelihood of a successful transplant in this case.
- Design a general model designed to facilitate other such transplants.

INSTRUCTIONS

Read the following message and answer the Question on p. 127.

PascO-OrwaN is a New York-based multinational that designs and manufactures tools.

There has been concern about the efficiency and motivation of headquarters staff. Specifically, many employees find their tasks too simple and repetitive, and feel unfulfilled by the work. This situation has been worsened by poor communication between departments, and too many levels of bureaucracy. Mobility is high; few managers stay with the company for longer than five years, and among the workforce average tenure is even shorter.

On the recommendation of a firm of management consultants, Barrett Brothers, the company has decided to implement a management system known as Structural Re-configuration (SR-c).

STRUCTURAL RE-CONFIGURATION

SR-c has developed as a version of systems re-engineering. It is not intended to simply enhance existing structures; rather, it discards them and replaces them with entirely new ones. In this sense SR-c serves as a tool for making radical change. Barrett Brothers say

> SR-c teams don't look for marginal benefits, but order of magnitude improvements. Making temporary adjustments to the old systems is not enough.

A Structural Re-configuration must be implemented across all target units in the company at the same time, and completed within four months. If the process is dragged out, discrepancies arise in the practice of different units. This immediacy is painful, but in the long term pays dividends.

SR-c focuses on changing the organizational structure so that series of related jobs can be combined and performed in their natural order – which may mean they are performed simultaneously. If a series of jobs can be performed in a continuous rather than interrupted process, needs for checks and controls are reduced. This reduction has two major effects.

First, it means that boundaries between organizational departments can be eliminated whenever possible. When greater speed and efficiency is demanded, work processes may be restructured so that departments can be merged. Second, this merging reduces the need for departmental supervisors and managers. The possibilities for reducing managerial staff numbers is greater when instructions, resourcing information, check processes and other processes are communicated through information technology.

Information technology drastically reduces the need for managerial expertise. The sort of manager who is needed under the new system is not the dedicated expert – because the computer gives you the expertise needed, and more efficiently – but rather the generalist with computational skills. Decision-making and planning now become the responsibilities of anyone with access to a database and computer skills.

In sum, SR-c has the effects of breaking down functional groups and of reducing the hierarchy, so flattening and simplifying the structure. Managers stop acting like supervisors and behave more like coaches, and fewer of them are required to command and control. Workers focus more on the customer's needs and less on the bosses'.

Research conducted by Barrett Brothers in New York and across the US northeast shows that employees are motivated by:

- greater opportunities to control their own work processes
- the reduction of detailed control by managers

The implementation of SR-c means that many PascO-OrwaN employees are bound to lose their jobs. Redundancies include supervisors and middle managers when the company is down-sized and flattened, and members of the workforce unable or acquire the new skills needed to use the technology. This is unfortunate. But labor is extremely expensive and the redundancies will make a major saving.

Those who survive and acquire new skills earn pay rises and promotions. Their work is more varied, and one employee spoke for the great majority when he said:

The job is more interesting now. I used to be doing the same production job all the time. Now I work with designers and even the marketing people, and I see all sides of the business. I'm being challenged to learn new skills and interact with people I haven't spoken to before. I know that if I screw up badly I can lose my job at any moment, but I can live with that. If anything, it adds excitement.

Those made redundant are helped find new work. Employees seem willing to accept the greater risks and uncertainty when the financial rewards are greater. Top management prizes the greater efficiency and enhanced capacity to serve customers. Barrett Brothers explain the success of their business revolution:

SR-c capitalizes on the same characteristics that have always made our people such great innovators: individualism, self-reliance, an acceptance of risk and a willingness to change.

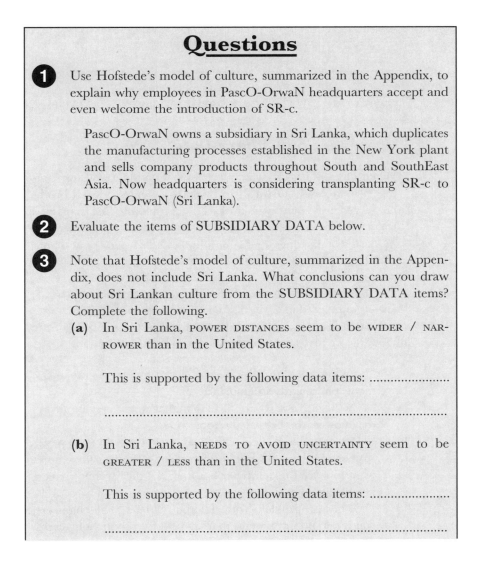

Questions

1 Use Hofstede's model of culture, summarized in the Appendix, to explain why employees in PascO-OrwaN headquarters accept and even welcome the introduction of SR-c.

PascO-OrwaN owns a subsidiary in Sri Lanka, which duplicates the manufacturing processes established in the New York plant and sells company products throughout South and SouthEast Asia. Now headquarters is considering transplanting SR-c to PascO-OrwaN (Sri Lanka).

2 Evaluate the items of SUBSIDIARY DATA below.

3 Note that Hofstede's model of culture, summarized in the Appendix, does not include Sri Lanka. What conclusions can you draw about Sri Lankan culture from the SUBSIDIARY DATA items? Complete the following.
(a) In Sri Lanka, POWER DISTANCES seem to be WIDER / NARROWER than in the United States.

This is supported by the following data items: ....

....

(b) In Sri Lanka, NEEDS TO AVOID UNCERTAINTY seem to be GREATER / LESS than in the United States.

This is supported by the following data items: ....

....

(c)   In Sri Lanka, relationships seem to be MORE INDIVIDUALIST / MORE COLLECTIVIST than in the United States.

This is supported by the following data items: ....

....

4 Given your answers to Question 3, do you expect the implementation of SR-c in Sri Lanka to achieve the same results as in the New York headquarters?
YES / NO.

5 What problems might arise in implementing SR-c in Sri Lanka?

....

....

....

....

Subsidiary Data

When PascO-OrwaN (headquarters) first considered transplanting SR-c to PascO-OrwaN (Sri Lanka), they hired Barrett Brothers to research the possibilities. The consultants first explained the principles and practice of SR-c to all Sri Lankan employees in a series of meetings, and later interviewed 62 persons at managerial and supervisory levels.

The following data items were excerpted from these interviews. They are numbered in terms of interviewee sequence. This numeration is otherwise random, and does not reflect the seniority of the interviewee or the perceived worth of his/her contribution.

1   "I am interested in SR-c because it is a new idea in management, particularly in globalization."

2a   "Whether or not we use a new management system always depends on the boss at the top."

2b   "Most of our staff stick to the way they worked in the past."

4   "When you have SR-c a lot of people will suffer. They don't want to learn the computer but they feel they will not have a job [if they don't]."

8   "We have a problem with different experts. The engineers, computer programmers, market people, production teams,

and so on, they all think they are the top people in the company and will not work with the others."

11a   "People see change and get scared. They think they will lose their jobs, that kind of thing."

11b   "Sometimes the culture of the foreigner cannot be adapted and Sri Lankan people cannot accept it. Some parts of SR-c can be applied in our PascO-OrwaN but I don't believe that all of it can work. We need to examine the ideas carefully before we decide what works for us."

11c   "The problem with trying to re-engineer here is that all the consultants who do the SR-c come in from America, they don't understand local culture."

15   "People get used to what they have done before. They get used to power, they get used to layers of hierarchy, they like to know their place in it."

20   "In our country we don't expect to dismiss staff. The most we do is transfer them to a subsidiary."

21   "It takes time. You can't reconfigure all sections of the structure together."

22   "I suppose that if the senior managers say we must reconfigure our company, we have to do what they say."

32   "Some companies want a complete revolution. But we change every day. I see the improvement every day. We don't need SR-c."

34   "Why do they want to use SR-c here? What is the strategic goal?"

35a   "Structural reconfiguration in Sri Lanka is not the same as in the West. Culture is a factor. In a Sri Lankan company if a worker has been with you for 20 years can you fire him without emotion in your mind? You have to find him another job, perhaps in another of your companies."

35b   "Old people may resist change."

38   "In Sri Lanka you have to convince people and you have to know how to adjust to the [cultural] environment."

40   "It sounds quite interesting. But I don't understand."

41   "Why are we always told to change by foreign consultants? But we might accept it if our own Sri Lankan consultants explained what we have to do, and showed patience if we make mistakes."

43   "Maybe it cannot work in a company here because it should change the structure and the people, and most of our people follow the old [strategy] of preferring to make small, small improvements but SR-c seems to mean change everything. At least, that's what I understand from the lesson you gave us."

47   "I'm not interested in radical change. I want to change small things, the interface between departments and between departments and customers."

48   "Top management haven't made us understand why we need to use SR-c in our company."

49   "Our people will accept everything, so if you can convince them you can do everything."

53   "Employees are worried that machines will replace them. So the management must explain that the computers will support their jobs, not replace their jobs. . . . If management does this, it should be okay."

54   "If we . . . reconfigure all departments at the same time we will upset a lot of old people. We have to start in marketing where people are younger and finish in production where people are older."

57   "A big problem is getting people to work together. Each department wants to keep out the others. We don't communicate between departments except when the top managers meet. Marketing, R&D, engineering, production – they do not have good relationships. Nobody has shown them out to work together."

59   "If I want to have my own ideas, I must try not to disagree with my boss. I have read the newspapers that say it is possible in other countries for subordinates to tell their superiors how to solve problems, but not in companies here."

60a "In Sri Lankan culture people are used to looking up and waiting to be told what to do. That makes SR-c difficult."

60b "In all Sri Lankan companies including our company it is very difficult to communicate with the big boss. He's too far away, we don't often see him."

61   "You have to change their habits. Our people take things very easily and have to be trained to take things seriously, before you can change the structure."

6 Discuss your analysis with other members of the class.

7 What GENERAL principles can you draw about planning how to transplant a management system from headquarters to a foreign subsidiary?
- Decide which of the following are important when making a transplant, but select ten only.
  (a) Reviewing the company's strategic goals.
       IMPORTANT / NOT IMPORTANT

  (b) Collecting information about the system and how it is implemented in its indigenous context (that is, the context

in which it was first developed – in the case of SR-c, PascO-OrwaN in New York).
IMPORTANT / NOT IMPORTANT

(c) Analysing the system; how does it reflect cultural and other factors characteristics of its indigenous context?
IMPORTANT / NOT IMPORTANT

(d) Telling subsidiary employees how the system is implemented within its indigenous context.
IMPORTANT / NOT IMPORTANT

(e) Communicating the adapted system within the subsidiary, as appropriate.
IMPORTANT / NOT IMPORTANT

(f) Analyzing the cultural context of the subsidiary. What factors will affect affect implementation of the system?
IMPORTANT / NOT IMPORTANT

(g) Implementing the system within the subsidiary.
IMPORTANT / NOT IMPORTANT

(h) Planning to adapt the system so that it is appropriate to the subsidiary context.
IMPORTANT / NOT IMPORTANT

(i) Planning any training necessary within the indigenous context.
IMPORTANT / NOT IMPORTANT

(j) Planning any training necessary to help implementation of the system within the subsidiary.
IMPORTANT / NOT IMPORTANT

(k) Training subsidiary top management.
IMPORTANT / NOT IMPORTANT

(l) Monitoring implementation of the system within the subsidiary, and depending on the outcomes of monitoring, modifying the system as necessary.
IMPORTANT / NOT IMPORTANT

(m) Defining your aim in transplanting the system, and reviewing how this helps achieve strategic goals.
IMPORTANT / NOT IMPORTANT

(n) Monitoring implementation of the system within the indigenous context.
IMPORTANT / NOT IMPORTANT

8 What support for your selection can you find in the data items? Complete the following.

My selection of (   ) is supported by item(s) ....

My selection of (   ) is supported by item(s) ....

My selection of (   ) is supported by item(s) ....

My selection of (   ) is supported by item(s) ....

My selection of (   ) is supported by item(s) ....

9 List the ten steps that you chose in Question 7. List them in the order that have to be performed when transplanting a management system from headquarters to a foreign subsidiary.

Complete the following:
WHEN TRANSPLANTING A MANAGEMENT SYSTEM FROM HEADQUARTERS TO SUBSIDIARY

The FIRST stage is ....

The SECOND stage is ....

The THIRD stage is ....

The FOURTH stage is ....

The FIFTH stage is ....

The SIXTH stage is ....

The SEVENTH stage is ....

The EIGHTH stage is..

The NINTH stage is..

The TENTH stage is ....

10 Your answer to Question 8 should give you a model for transplanting. Discuss your answer with other members of the class.

the Ruritanian Electronics negotiation

> AIM: This project gives practice in negotiating in circumstances where cultural differences are significant.
>
> Specifically, Project 6 asks you to:
>
> - Read case materials.
> - Prepare to negotiate a wage settlement.
> - Negotiate.
> - Report on your negotiation.
>
> To the INSTRUCTOR: Notes on organizing the negotiation are given in section S at the end of this project.

Instructions

Ruritanian Electronics

BACKGROUND

A Ruritanian Electronics manufactures computer components. It is based in the Republic of Ruritania.

B All management personnel are Ruritanian. There are no Ruritanians in the workforce, which has been entirely recruited from two immigrant populations: the Abadabinese and the Feefifofians.

    The Abadabinese make up 50 percent of the workforce; the Feefifofians make up 50 percent of the workforce.

C The Abadabinese and the Feefifofians have very different cultures (see Cultural profiles, below). Nevertheless, they usually work together in harmony. This communal harmony is a source of pride to top management.

D By Ruritanian law, management must negotiate an annual labor contract with the workforce. That time has now come round.

E The negotiation is conducted in groups, each of three persons. They are:
- the Personnel Manager (a Ruritanian)
- the Abadabinese representative
- the Feefifofian representative

F When they have completed their negotiation, the group prepare a presentation, summarizing and explaining their settlement.

G The Personnel Manager aims to negotiate the best possible deal for the company – but not at the expense of communal harmony.

If you secure a good deal (which costs the company little), you may be promoted to the board. If you do not secure a good deal, you are in danger of losing your job. (The teacher will tell you before the negotiation how many points you must earn to be promoted or sacked.)

If your negotiation does not reach settlement within the time allowed, you lose your job. If your negotiation leads to a breakdown in good relations between the Abadabinese and Feefifofian communities, you lose your job and probably go to prison.

H Each of the Abadabinese and Feefifofian representatives aims to negotiate:
- as good a deal as possible for the workforce
- as good a deal as possible for his/her own community

None of the three is likely to get as much as he or she wants. Each has to negotiate an agreement with the other two, who have their own, different, interests.

When you negotiate, prioritize your demands on the basis of your community's cultural needs. When you come to report the negotiation (see R below), you will need to justify your negotiating position to your community. If you get good terms, you are treated as a hero of your community and the best schools receive your children. If you get poor terms, you lose your friends and have to educate your children at home.

Cultural profiles

I ABADABINESE culture
Compared to Feefifofian culture, power distances are narrow. Needs to avoid uncertainty are low. Masculine assertiveness is respected. Relations to others are individualist, and non-comformity is greatly valued as an indication of strength of character. The individual who sacrifices his or her personal freedom in the interests of group conformity is perceived to be a "wimp".

Hofstede's model for comparing cultures (summarized in the Appendix) should give you more ideas about a typical culture that fits this profile.

Typical sayings in Abadabinese culture include: "Running ahead of the crowd is strength. Walking with the crowd is weakness." "Woman is the back legs of a fighting bear." "The hero burns the bridges behind him." The Abadabinese value material wealth, but this is not their only priority and often not their main priority.

J   FEEFIFOFIAN culture

Compared to Feefifofian culture, power distances are wide. Needs to avoid uncertainty are high. Feminine tenderness is respected and "macho" behavior is considered vulgar. Relations to others are collectivist, and non-comformity is considered dangerous to the individual (who rejects society's support systems) and to the group.

Hofstede's model for comparing cultures (summarized in the Appendix) should give you more ideas about a typical culture that fits this profile.

Typical sayings in Feefifofian culture include: "Walking with the crowd is strength. Running ahead of the crowd is weakness." "Man is the front legs of a dancing horse." "The fool burns the bridges behind him." The Feefifofians value material wealth, but this is not their only priority and often not their main priority.

K   RURITANIAN culture

Ruritanian values are midway between Abadabinese and Feefifofian values. Power distances are moderate, needs to avoid uncertainty are moderate, individualism is moderate, feminity is moderate.

Ruritanian culture does not have any typical sayings.

PREPARATION

L   The class divides into groups of three, each consisting of a Personnel Manager, an Abadabinese, a Feefifofian. (If no precise division can be made, one or two of these roles might be played by two students.

M   Each group MUST reach a single settlement. That is, the Personnel Manager MUST NOT strike single deals with the two communal representatives.

N   Prepare by:

- all Personnel Managers meeting to discuss their interest sheet (Interest Sheet 1, below) and agreeing on a general position.
- all Abadabinese representatives meeting to discuss their interest sheet (Interest Sheet 2, below) and agreeing on a general position.
- all Feefifofian representatives meeting to discuss their interest sheet (Interest Sheet 3, below) and agreeing on a general position.

ABADABINESE AND FEEFIFOFIAN INTEREST SHEETS

O Read the Item list below. Use this in negotiation. Focus on negotiating good terms on those Items that are most likely to meet your
community's needs. Which Items are these? Base your decision on
your cultural profile and your interpretation of the Appendix.

P For each of the three items, your group MUST settle on one of a–e.

Item: PAY (assuming inflation at 3 percent this year)

   (a) A 10 percent pay rise for all.

   (b) A 15 percent pay rise for the 10 percent most productive individuals; 10 percent for the next fifty
percent; 5 percent for all others.

   (c) An 8 percent pay rise for all.

   (d) A 9 percent pay rise for the 30 percent most productive; 3 percent for all others.

   (e) A 2 percent pay rise for all.

Item: CONTRACTS

   (a) All contracts to be negotiated on an individual basis;
no contracts longer than three years.

   (b) Ten-year contracts for the 10 percent most productive.

   (c) Five-year contracts for all.

   (d) Lifetime contracts for the 20 percent most senior (seniority measured in terms of years worked for the company), 10-year contracts for the next ten percent most
senior, 3-year contracts for the next 40 percent.

   (e) Lifetime contracts for the 80 percent most productive.

Item: RECOGNITION OF ACHIEVEMENT

   (a) Achievement awards of one years pay paid to the top
10 percent most productive individuals; awards of
two months pay paid to the next 30 percent.

   (b) A weekend-break in a local luxury hotel awarded to
all employees achieving satisfactorily and with more
than one year's service.

   (c) Achievement awards (eight months pay) paid to the
top 5 percent most productive groups.

   (d) Top 30 percent most productive achievers rewarded
with decorative plaques and official dinners.

   (e) Letters of thanks sent to all employees completing
three years of satisfactory service; no other recognition
of achievement.

PERSONNEL MANAGER'S INTEREST SHEETS

Q Together with the Abadabinese and Feefifofian representatives you
negotiate the following (see above).

Note that points are given against each Item below. You hope to negotiate for as LOW A TOTAL AS POSSIBLE. Low points indicate terms that are cheap for the company.

A total of only 7 points guarantees your promotion to the board and a massive pay rise. If you score at this level, well done! A very expensive total of 18 points guarantees that your dismissal from the company. Goodbye!

THE INSTRUCTOR WILL CHOOSE THE PRECISE RE-WARD/PUNISHMENT SCORESHEET FOR YOU!

For each Item, your group MUST settle on one of a–e.

Item: PAY   POINTS

    (a)   A 10 percent pay rise for all.   9

    (b)   A 15 percent pay rise for the 10 percent most productive individuals; 10 percent for the next fifty percent; 5 percent for all others.   7

    (c)   An 8 percent pay rise for all.   5

    (d)   A 9 percent pay rise for the thirty percent most productive; 3 percent for all others.   3

    (e)   A 2 percent pay rise for all.   1

Item: CONTRACTS

    (a)   All contracts to be negotiated on an individual basis; no contracts longer than 3-year.   1

    (b)   Ten-year contracts for the 10 percent most productive.   4

    (c)   Five-year contracts for all.   6

    (d)   Lifetime contracts for the 20 percent most senior (seniority measured in terms of years worked for the company), 10-year contracts for the next ten percent most senior, 3-year contracts for the next 40 percent.   7

    (e)   Lifetime contracts for the 80 percent of the most productive employees.   10

Item: RECOGNITION OF ACHIEVEMENT

    (a)   Achievement awards of one year's pay paid to the top 10 percent most productive individuals; awards of two months pay paid to the next 30 percent.   8

    (b)   A weekend-break in a local luxury hotel awarded to all employees achieving satisfactorily and with more than one year's service.   6

    (c)   Achievement awards (8 months' pay) paid to the top 5 percent most productive groups.   5

   (d)   Top 30 percent most productive achievers
          rewarded with decorative plaques and official
          dinners.   2

   (e)   Letters of thanks sent to all employees
          completing three years of satisfactory service;
          no other recognition of achievement.   0

R   POST-NEGOTIATION

1   In your group, prepare a presentation reporting the terms of
    your settlemement. Explain your considerations in reaching
    the settlement.

2   Present your settlement.

S   Instructor's Notes

1   Divide the class into groups of three. When this material is
    used with a culturally diverse class, try to ensure a wide spread
    of cultures.

2   Check that students understand the situation and their roles.

3   Set a time limit within which the negotiation should be
    completed.

4   Select a Reward/Punishment Scoresheet from the following
    and tell the personnel managers that this should guide their
    choice of negotiation tactics. It must NOT be shared with the
    Abadabinese and Feefifofians.

    REWARD/PUNISHMENT SCORESHEET A:

    2–6 points   :   You are promoted to the board and given a
                     generous pay rise.
    7–12   :   No promotion; generous pay rise.
    13–16   :   Small pay rise.
    17–19   :   No pay rise, but you keep your job.
    20–22   :   You keep your job on probation.
    23–27   :   Instant dismissal.

    REWARD/PUNISHMENT SCORESHEET B:

    2–4 points   :   You are promoted to the board and given a
                     generous pay rise.
    5–13   :   Small pay rise and a new company car.
    14–22   :   No pay rise, but you keep your job.
    23–27   :   Immediate dismissal.

    REWARD/PUNISHMENT SCORESHEET C:

    2–9 points   :   You are promoted to the board and given a
                     generous pay rise.
    10–29   :   Generous pay rise and car and housing
                     allowances.
    20–27   :   Instant dismissal.

    REWARD/PUNISHMENT SCORESHEET D:

    (The instructor decides)

workplace
communication:
needs analysis

AIM: This project gives practice in analysing communication functions performed at work/study, and develops understanding of how good communication skills contribute to successful performance of work.

This project is designed for students who have (or have recently had) a job.
Specifically, Project 7 asks you to:

- Analyze the communicative functions that you perform at work.
- Identify communicative priorities.
- Apply the findings to analyzing the communicative needs of a non-native
speaker doing the same job.

Instructions

1. Suppose that you have been promised promotion from your present
job (or the job you last held), and a foreigner who speaks some
other native language has been hired as your successor to perform
precisely the same job.

2. This foreigner has a reasonable command of the grammar and
vocabulary of your language; but he/she has little experience of
communicating with native speakers.

3. You have been asked to make a communicative needs analysis of
your job.

4. This needs analysis will be used to design a syllabus of training
materials. The syllabus will train your successor in the communicative skills needed.

5 Complete this questionnaire:

(a) How much of your working time do you devote to using ORAL skills (speaking, listening) and how much to TEXT skills (reading, writing) – in percentages?

    (i)   speaking ....%   (ii)   listening ....%

    (iii) reading ....%   (iv) writing ....%

(b) How important are these ORAL and TEXT skills? Rank them, from 1 (most important) to 4 (least important).

    (i)   speaking ....   (ii)   listening ....

    (iii) reading ....   (iv) writing ....

(c) HOW MUCH of your working TIME do you spend in communicating with each of the following groups – in percentages?

    A   Superiors   ....%

    B   People on the same level as you   ....%

    C   People on a lower level than you   ....%

    D   Customers and suppliers   ....%

    E   Other persons outside the company ....%

(d) How much of your working time do you spend in communicating with the five groups listed above using ORAL skills and TEXT skills – in percentages?

    A   Superiors   .....% (ORAL .....%, TEXT ......%)

    B   People on the same level .....% (ORAL .....%, TEXT ......%)

    C   People on a lower level .....% (ORAL .....%, TEXT ......%)

    D   Customer and suppliers .....% (ORAL .....%, TEXT ......%)

    E   Other persons outside
        the company   .....% (ORAL .....%, TEXT ......%)

(e) Review your answers to (d) above. How IMPORTANT is it that you communicate effectively with each of the five groups, using either set of skills? Rank the following, using [1] for the most important, and [10] for the least important.

    A1.   Superiors,   using ORAL skills.   [ ]

    A2.   Superiors,   using TEXT skills.   [ ]

    B1.   People on the same level,   using ORAL skills.   [ ]

    B2.   People on the same level,   using TEXT skills.   [ ]

    C1.   People on a lower LEVEL, using ORAL skills.   [ ]

    C2.   People on a lower LEVEL, using TEXT skills.   [ ]

    D1.   Customers and suppliers,   using ORAL skills.   [ ]

    D2.   Customers and suppliers,   using TEXT skills.   [ ]

    E1.   Other outsiders,   using ORAL skills.   [ ]

    E2.   Other outsiders,   using TEXT skills.   [ ]

(f) Now prioritize the SIX most important group-skill profiles (underlining your choice of A . . . E):

    [1] is A1 / A2 / B1 / B2 / C1 / C2 / D1 / D2 / E1 / E2

    [2] is A1 / A2 / B1 / B2 / C1 / C2 / D1 / D2 / E1 / E2

[3] is A1 / A2 / B1 / B2 / C1 / C2 / D1 / D2 / E1 / E2
[4] is A1 / A2 / B1 / B2 / C1 / C2 / D1 / D2 / E1 / E2
[5] is A1 / A2 / B1 / B2 / C1 / C2 / D1 / D2 / E1 / E2
[6] is A1 / A2 / B1 / B2 / C1 / C2 / D1 / D2 / E1 / E2

(g) For each of your six choices in (f), decide which three SUB-SKILLS are most important, and complete the table below. Oral SUB-SKILLS; communicating (producing and responding) in

(i)   one-on-one meetings.
(ii)   small-group meetings.
(iii) conferences.
(iv)   presentations.
(v)   telephone.
(vi)   voice mail.
(vii) (any other ....)

Text SUB-SKILLS: communicating (producing and responding) in

(viii) e-mail.
(ix)   inter-office memos.
(x)   faxes.
(xi)   Post-It notes.
(xii) pager messages.
(xiii) reports.
(xiv) letters.
(xv)   (any other ....)

For communicating with my prioritized group-profiles, I prioritize the following SUB-SKILLS':
priority: group profile:
[1]   : A1 / A2 / B1 / B2 / C1 / C2 / D1 / D2 / E1 / E2
prioritized sub-skills are   (1) .... (2) .... (3) ....
[2]   : .... ; sub-skills are   (1) .... (2) .... (3) ....
[3]   : .... ; sub-skills are   (1) .... (2) .... (3) ....
[4]   : .... ; sub-skills are   (1) .... (2) .... (3) ....
[5]   : .... ; sub-skills are   (1) .... (2) .... (3) ....
[6]   : .... ; sub-skills are   (1) .... (2) .... (3) ....

(h) Now decide which workplace FUNCTIONS you need to communicate with each of your prioritized group profiles:

(i)   lead.
(ii)   respond to leadership.
(iii) liaise.
(iv)   respond to liaison.
(v)   monitor.
(vi)   respond to monitoring.
(vii) disseminate information.

(viii)   respond to information.

(ix)   plan.

(x)   respond to planning.

(xi)   act as spokesperson.

(xii)   respond to a spokesperson.

(xiii) control.

(xiv)   respond to control.

(xv)   resolve conflict.

(xvi)   respond to conflict resolution.

(xvii) allocate resources.

(xviii) respond to resource allocation.

(xix)   negotiate.

(xx)   propose new ideas.

(xxi)   respond to new ideas.

(xxii) (any other: ....)

(i)   You should now be able to write six sentences describing your communicative priorities. Here is an example.

"My first priority is to communicate with (A) superiors, communicating in (SUB-SKILL) one-on-one meetings in order to (FUNCTION) respond to control."

1   My first priority is to communicate with (A)
.... communicating in (SUB-SKILL)
....in order to (FUNCTION)
....

2   My second priority is to communicate with (A)
.... communicating in (SUB-SKILL)
....in order to (FUNCTION)
....

3   My third priority is to communicate with (A)
.... communicating in (SUB-SKILL)
....in order to (FUNCTION)
....

4   My fourth priority is to communicate with (A)
.... communicating in (SUB-SKILL)
....in order to (FUNCTION)
....

5   My fifth priority is to communicate with (A)
.... communicating in (SUB-SKILL)
....in order to (FUNCTION)
....

6   My sixth priority is to communicate with (A)
.... communicating in (SUB-SKILL)
....in order to (FUNCTION)
....

6 Check your answers to (i) with other persons who perform a similar role in your organization.

7 Use the information that you have collected above to prepare a presentation. This reports on your job, and the communication skills needed to perform the job efficiently. The foreigner coming into your job needs to perform these communicative skills. Which of these skills might be most difficult for a non-native speaker?

8 Make the presentation.

APPENDIX: HOFSTEDE'S MODEL

CULTURE DEFINED

Many different definitions of culture have been made. That given here is common in management literature. Culture is defined as:

> the collective programming of the mind which distinguishes the members of one human group from another. . . . Culture, in this sense, includes systems of values and values are the building blocks of culture. (Hofstede, 1984, p. 21)

This implies that:

- a culture is particular to one group and not to others. The values are shared to varying degrees by all members.

   In this book we are chiefly concerned with national cultures, and so the national group is the typical unit of analysis. However, other culture groups can be observed:

   sub-national cultures;

   industry cultures (e.g., the cultures of banking, supermarket retailing, the auto industry, etc.);

   organizational cultures (the cultures of Coca Cola, the Bank of England, BMW, a Hong Kong family company);

   gender cultures;

   generational cultures;

   class cultures.

- a culture influences the behavior of group members in uniform and predictable ways. This means that the manager who understands the cultural values of the workforce can make some predictions of how they will behave in routine situations.

- a culture is learned and not innate. No one is born with instinctive understanding of his or her culture. Rather, it is handed down from one generation to the next.

One starts learning culture (in particular language) in very early child-hood. Typically, an individual first learns from parents and other family members, then from friends, school, the media. The roles played by these different agencies seems to vary in different national cultures.

- culture includes systems of values; these are defined below.

VALUES

Values are defined as assumptions of how people should behave. The individual may never be able to fully articulate his or her culture. Because so much culture is acquired in childhood at a preconscious level, it is deeply engrained and your root values are slow to change. Because they are held in the unconscious mind, values influence behavior in ways that the individual takes for granted and does not challenge. Case 1 gives an example.

Values may correspond with conscious attitudes and beliefs, but these often give an unreliable guide towards true values. The individual may claim beliefs that he or she fails to express in practice. For example, almost every modern manager believes in the importance of good communication and hopes to be a good communicator. But in practice, the behavior of many does not meet the ideal. We have all met the manager who says "my office door is open at any time" but never has the time to listen to YOUR complaint, or if he or she listens, never has time to resolve YOUR problem.

In general, behavior rather than good intentions reveals values.

HOFSTEDE'S MODEL (1980, 1984, 1997)

The model of culture most used in management studies is that designed by Geert Hofstede. Hofstede first developed it in 1980. Since then he has discussed its implications in a range of academic papers and books, most recently in Hofstede (1997); but the fundamentals have not been changed. Many scholars have tested the model since 1980 and in general support its findings. Evidence collected twenty years after the original research finds few signs of significant change in relations between the cultures. No other study matches the model for scope and rigor. Its strengths and weaknesses are discussed in Mead 1998.

Hofstede investigated the values held by 116,000 employees at different categories (from unskilled to managers of professional workers) in branches and affiliates of IBM, in 50 countries and three regions. The regions are:

- the Arab region; consisting of Egypt, Iraq, Kuwait, Lebanon, Saudi Arabia.
- the East African region; consisting of Ethiopa, Kenya, Tanzania, Zambia.
- the West African region; consisting of Ghana, Nigeria, Sierra Leone.

Hofstede sorted the findings derived from his questionnaire into four dimensions:

- POWER DISTANCE: the distance between individuals at different levels of a hierarchy.
- UNCERTAINTY AVOIDANCE: more or less need to avoid uncertainty about the future and in work relationships.
- INDIVIDUALISM versus COLLECTIVISM: the relationships that the individual has with other people.
- MASCULINITY versus FEMINITY: the division of roles and values in society.

Hofstede's model is COMPARATIVE and is used to compare one national culture against another. It does not set up absolutes. Thus we would be incorrect to say, for example, that Peru has a high power distance culture. Rather, Peruvian power distances are high compared to those of the United States but low compared to those of Indonesia – just as power distances in the United States are higher than those of Austria, and Indonesia power distances are lower than those of Malaysia.

This point is important because some users try to simplify the model by distinguishing on a bilateral basis – for example, distinguishing high power distance cultures and low power distance cultures. In practice, all are ranked on a continuum.

Second, the fact that all informants worked for IBM indicates that even a powerful multinational is unable to impose the same values on all its members in different countries. The national culture always influences how members express the values of their organization, and how they experience the organizational culture.

The meanings of the four dimensions, as summarized below, are derived mainly from Hofstede (1997), otherwise from Hofstede (1994).

POWER DISTANCES

The dimension of power distance deals with the desirability or not of social inequality. It demonstrates how the culture group adapts to inequalities among its members.

In all societies there are hierarchies. The clever have more power than the stupid, the healthy have more power than the stupid, the young middle-aged have more power than the very young and the very old. Some cultures accept and even reinforce these differences in power; the rich have greater access to political power, and can pay for better education and better health-care. They find it easier to avoid paying tax. Other cultures try to narrow these differences, for example by making good education and health care available to other, and by taxing the rich.

When power distances are relatively high, hierarchical differences are more respected. Managers are expected to make decisions autocratically and paternalistically. Less powerful people should be dependent on the more powerful. In the workplace, subordinates expect to be told what to do and the ideal boss is expected to be a benevolent autocrat or good parent. Organizations are often highly centralized under the control of a boss who tries to look as impressive as possible and whose word is seldom challenged. All aspects of society stress hierarchy and strati-fication rather than equality. Organizational hierarchies reflect perceptions that higher-up persons are naturally superior to lower-downs.

In cultures where power distances are relatively low, the opposite connotations apply. Decentralization is popular and subordinates expect to be consulted. Status symbols are frowned upon. Organizational hierarchies indicate inequalities in roles. That is, the managing role is perceived as more important than an assistant's role – but this does not mean that the person occupying the senior role is naturally a superior person.

Table 1 shows that power distances are greatest in Malaysia, and least in Austria.

Table 1 Power distance index (PDI) values for 50 countries and three regions

Score rank	Country of region	PDI score	Score rank	Country or region	PDI score
1	Malaysia	104	27/28	South Korea	60
2/3	Guatemala	95	29/30	Iran	58
2/3	Panama	95	29/30	Taiwan	58
4	Philippines	94	31	Spain	57
5/6	Mexico	81	32	Pakistan	55
5/6	Venezuela	81	33	Japan	54
7	Arab countries	80	34	Italy	50
8/9	Equador	78	35/36	Argentina	49
8/9	Indonesia	78	35/36	South Africa	49
10/11	India	77	37	Jamaica	45
10/11	West Africa	77	38	USA	40
12	Yugoslavia	76	39	Canada	39
13	Singapore	74	40	Netherlands	38
14	Brazil	69	41	Australia	36
15/16	France	68	42/44	Costa Rica	35
15/16	Hong Kong	68	42/44	Germany FR	35
17	Colombia	67	42/44	Great Britain	35
18/19	Salvador	66	45	Switzerland	34
18/19	Turkey	66	46	Finland	33
20	Belgium	65	47/48	Norway	31
21/23	East Africa	64	47/48	Sweden	31
21/23	Peru	64	49	Ireland (Republic of)	28
21/23	Thailand	64	50	New Zealand	22
24/25	Chile	63	51	Denmark	18
24/25	Portugal	63	52	Israel	13
26	Uruguay	61	53	Austria	11
27/28	Greece	60			

Source: Geert Hofstede, *Cultures and Organizations: Software of the Mind* (New York: McGraw-Hill, 1997), p. 26.

UNCERTAINTY AVOIDANCE

In all societies, life is uncertain. No one can be entirely certain of the future, or about relationships with others. This dimension measures how far cultures socialize their members into tolerating uncertainty about the future and about ambiguous situations.

In cultures that have higher needs to avoid uncertainty, the uncertainty inherent in life is felt as a continuous threat which must be fought. Members of these cultures suffer higher anxiety and higher job stress and are less ready to take risks. Familiar risks may be accepted, but innovation is treated as potentially dangerous, and change is resisted.

Members appear anxiety prone and devote considerable energy to "beating the future" and in the workplace place a premium on job security, career patterning, retirements and health insurance. Clear rules and regulations are expected. The manager issues clear instructions and subordinates are given little opportunity for initiative. Managers should be expert in their technical fields rather than generalists who facilitate.

In cultures where needs to avoid uncertainty are relatively low, the opposite connotations apply and members show tolerance of greater degrees of ambiguity. Table 2 shows that needs to avoid uncertainty are greatest in Greece, and least in Singapore.

Table 2 Uncertainty avoidance index (UAI) values for 50 countries and three regions

Score rank	Country or region	UAI score	Score rank	Country or region	UAI score
1	Greece	112	28	Equador	67
2	Portugal	104	29	Germany FR	65
3	Guatemala	101	30	Thailand	64
4	Uruguay	100	31/32	Iran	59
5/6	Belgium	94	31/32	Finland	59
5/6	Salvador	94	33	Switzerland	58
7	Japan	92	34	West Africa	54
8	Yugoslavia	88	35	Netherlands	53
9	Peru	87	36	East Africa	52
10/15	France	86	37	Australia	51
10/15	Chile	86	38	Norway	50
10/15	Spain	86	39/40	South Africa	49
10/15	Costa Rica	86	39/40	New Zealand	49
10/15	Panama	86	41/42	Indonesia	48
10/15	Argentina	86	41/42	Canada	48
16/17	Turkey	85	43	USA	46
16/17	South Korea	85	44	Philippines	44
18	Mexico	82	45	India	40
19	Israel	81	46	Malaysia	36
20	Colombia	80	47/48	Great Britain	35
21/22	Venezuela	76	47/48	Ireland (Republic of)	35
21/22	Brazil	76	49/50	Hong Kong	29
23	Italy	75	49/50	Sweden	29
24/25	Pakistan	70	51	Denmark	23
24/25	Austria	70	52	Jamaica	13
26	Taiwan	69	53	Singapore	8
27	Arab countries	68			

Source: as for table 1, p. 113.

INDIVIDUALISM *VERSUS* COLLECTIVISM

This dimension describes the relationship between the individual and the groups to which he or she belongs.

The more individualist cultures stress individual rights, achievements and responsibilities, and expect the individual to focus on satisfying his/her needs with relatively little regard to others. Competition is expected, and considered healthy. Individual decisions are valued over group decisions, and the individual has a greater right to thoughts and opinions which differ from those held by the majority. The manager aims for variety rather than conformity in work and does not have strong emotional connections with the company. He/she is loyal for as long as it suits his/her interests; that is, loyalty is calculative.

Individualism should not be automatically equated with greed – which occurs in any cultural context. Individualism and collectivism are better distinguished in terms of the social priorities that influence decision-making.

Table 3   Individualism index (IDV) values for 50 countries and three regions

Score rank	Country or region	IDV score	Score rank	Country or region	IDV score
1	USA	91	28	Turkey	37
2	Australia	90	29	Uruguay	36
3	Great Britain	89	30	Greece	35
4/5	Canada	80	31	Philippines	32
4/5	Netherlands	80	32	Mexico	30
6	New Zealand	79	33/35	East Africa	27
7	Italy	76	33/35	Yugoslavia	27
8	Belgium	75	33/35	Portugal	27
9	Denmark	74	36	Malaysia	26
10/11	Sweden	71	37	Hong Kong	25
10/11	France	71	38	Chile	23
12	Ireland (Republic of)	70	39/41	West Africa	20
13	Norway	69	39/41	Singapore	20
14	Switzerland	68	39/41	Thailand	20
15	Germany F.R.	67	42	Salvador	19
16	South Africa	65	43	South Korea	18
17	Finland	63	44	Taiwan	17
18	Austria	55	45	Peru	16
19	Israel	54	46	Costa Rica	15
20	Spain	51	47/48	Pakistan	14
21	India	48	47/48	Indonesia	14
22/23	Japan	46	49	Colombia	13
22/23	Argentina	46	50	Venezuela	12
24	Iran	41	51	Panama	11
25	Jamaica	39	52	Equador	8
26/27	Brazil	38	53	Guatemala	6
26/27	Arab countries	38			

Source: as for table 1, p. 53.

In the more collectivist cultures, groups interests prevail over individual interests, and the individual derives his social identity from the groups of which he or she is a member – including family, school class, work unit. Harmony should always be maintained within the group, although relations with competing groups may be distant. A high premium is placed on loyalty to group members, which may be valued above efficiency. The relationship between employer and employee is perceived in moral terms, like a family link. Hiring and promotion decisions take the individual's in-group into account.

Where individualism is low, collectivism is high, and where high, collectivism is low. No culture is entirely individualist or entirely collectivist. Even the United States, the most individualist culture, is collectivist in some respects – for instance, in college fraternities or in support for sports teams. Guatemelan culture is the most collectivist.

Table 4   Masculinity index (MAS) values for 50 countries and three regions

Score rank	Country or region	MAS score	Score rank	Country or region	MAS score
1	Japan	95	28	Singapore	48
2	Austria	79	29	Israel	47
3	Venezuela	73	30/31	Indonesia	46
4/5	Italy	70	30/31	West Africa	46
4/5	Switzerland	70	32/33	Turkey	45
6	Mexico	69	32/33	Taiwan	45
7/8	Ireland (Republic of)	68	34	Panama	44
7/8	Jamaica	68	35/36	Iran	43
9/10	Great Britain	66	35/36	France	43
9/10	Germany FR	66	37/38	Spain	42
11/12	Philippines	64	37/38	Peru	42
11/12	Colombia	64	39	East Africa	41
13/14	South Africa	63	40	Salvador	40
13/14	Equador	63	41	South Korea	39
15	USA	62	42	Uruguay	38
16	Australia	61	43	Guatemala	37
17	New Zealand	58	44	Thailand	34
18/19	Greece	57	45	Portugal	31
18/19	Hong Kong	57	46	Chile	28
20/21	Argentina	56	47	Finland	26
20/21	India	56	48/49	Yugoslavia	21
22	Belgium	54	48/49	Costa Rica	21
23	Arab countries	53	50	Denmark	16
24	Canada	52	51	Netherlands	14
25/26	Malaysia	50	52	Norway	8
25/26	Pakistan	50	53	Sweden	5
27	Brazil	49			

Source: as for table 1, p. 84.

MASCULINITY *VERSUS* FEMINITY

In the more masculine cultures, the social ideal is performance, and the maintenance of economic growth has top priority. Employees may give the company higher priority than the home. Material success and progress are dominant ideals. Big and fast are beautiful. There is sympathy for the strong and conflicts are resolved by fighting them out.

Sex roles are sharply differentiated. Some jobs may be more likely reserved for one sex rather than the other; for example, few men may be primary school teachers and few women politicians. Men are supposed to be competitive and assertive, women tender and able to take care of relationships.

In the more feminine cultures, the social ideal is welfare. The preservation of the environment should have the highest priority. Achievement is measured in terms of human contacts rather than of power and property. Small and slow are beautiful. There is sympathy for the outsider and the weak, and conflicts are resolved by negotiation.

Sex roles are less differentiated and both men and women are found in the highest ranks in all professions. Modesty in both sexes is valued. The company should not interfere in its employees' private lives.

Table 4 shows that Japanese culture is the most masculine, and Swedish the most feminine.

BIBLIOGRAPHY

Hofstede, Geert. 1980. *Culture's Consequences: International Differences in Work-Related Values.* Beverly Hills, CA: Sage.

Hofstede, Geert. 1984. *Culture's Consequences: International Differences in Work-Related Values.* Abridged edition. Beverly Hills, CA: Sage.

Hofstede, Geert. 1997. *Cultures and Organizations: Software of the Mind.* Revised edition. Maidenhead: McGraw-Hill.

Lever, Laurence. "£20m man who still goes by bus." *The Mail on Sunday*, April 16, 1995.

Manning, Clinton. "£20m a year? My man's worth every penny (even if he did lose £200m of his clients' money)." *Daily Mirror*, April 17, 1995.

Mead, Richard. 1998. *International Management: Cross-Cultural Dimensions.* Second edition. Oxford: Blackwell Publishers.

Oh, Seong Yeob. 1998. Model Hotel Management in Global Perspective: The Olympia Hotel in Ulsan, Korea. IFCOS independent study project, School of Oriental and African Studies, The University of London.

INDEX